ASTRID PROKOFIEFF-SEUFERT, born i[illegible] an interest in Rudolf Steiner's educationa[illegible] ied piano at the Academy of Music in Ba[illegible] at the Goetheanum, Switzerland. She met her husband in 1981 and supported him in his work for some 33 years. Since 2014, together with Hans Hasler, she founded the Sergej O. Prokofieff Archiv, managing and promoting the worldwide publication of her late husband's works.

HANS HASLER, born in 1942 in the Grison Swiss Alps, worked in special education in Switzerland and in a Camphill home in Finland. Later he worked for many years at the Goetheanum in various positions, including as leader of the building administration. He is co-director of the Sergej O. Prokofieff Archiv, and has lived in Finland since his retirement.

A LIFE FOR ANTHROPOSOPHY

Memories of Sergei O. Prokofieff

Edited by Astrid Prokofieff and Hans Hasler

TEMPLE LODGE

Temple Lodge Publishing Ltd.
Hillside House, The Square
Forest Row, RH18 5ES

www.templelodge.com

First published in English by Temple Lodge in 2025

Originally published in German under the title *Ein Leben für die Anthroposophie, Erinnerungen an Sergej O. Prokofieff* by Verlag am Goetheanum, Dornach, Switzerland, in 2023

Translation of the German and Russian contributions by Simon Blaxland-de Lange and the Spanish contribution by Ronja Eis. Unless otherwise indicated, all photographs are from the Sergei O. Prokofieff Archive

A CIP catalogue record for this book is available from the British Library

ISBN 978 1 915776 39 6

Cover by Morgan Creative. Image from summer 2009. (Sergei and Astrid spent many of their summer holidays in the dacha settlement of the Association of Russian Composers on the shore of Lake Lagoda. This possibility originated with Sergei's grandfather, Sergei Sergeyevich Prokofiev, and his uncle, the famous pianist Samuil Feinberg.)
Typeset by Symbiosys Technologies, Visakhapatnam, India
Printed and bound by 4Edge Ltd., Essex

Contents

Foreword 1

AUTOBIOGRAPHICAL
Sergei O. Prokofieff
33 Years as an Anthroposophical Author: an Overview 5
Brief Biography 5
A Perspective of the Future of the Anthroposophical Society and the Goetheanum 7

CHILDHOOD AND FAMILY
Sophia Leonidovna Prokofieva
Seryozha's Childhood and Youth 11
Valentina Chemberdzhi
Seryozha in the Circle of his Family 31
Katya Chemberdzhi
Memories of Childhood 43
Elena Abramova
Meeting in New Zealand 46

EARLY YEARS OF ANTHROPOSOPHICAL WORK IN THE UNDERGROUND, 1976–1981
Pyotr Alexandrovich Chaikovsky
A Friendship since the 1970s in Moscow 65
Georgi Kavtaradze
Some Cursory Notes of Meetings with Sergei Prokofieff 70
Dieter Hornemann
Work in the Underground, as experienced by a Foreigner 76
Peter Heusser
Memories of Journeys and Meetings with Sergei Prokofieff 79

1981–1985: FIRST JOURNEY AND RETURN
Astrid Prokofieff
Christmas 1981 in Dornach and a Turning-Point in Life 87

Heinrich Schneider
An Art Expedition to Moscow 99
Paul and Ulrike Mackay
Early Connections and Later Collaboration 101
Nicholas Nunhofer
Gifts of an East-European to People from the West 102
Sevak Edward Gulbekian
Reminiscences of Sergei O. Prokofieff 105

1985–2014: DORNACH, GERMANY, JOURNEYS
Virginia Sease
Sergei O. Prokofieff's Work in the Executive Council at the Goetheanum 113
Elisaveta Nikolayevna Gulbina
Memories of Sergei Prokofieff 121
Rolf Herzog
Life Encounters 125
Ulrike Drew
Motzstraβe Berlin 127
Astrid Prokofieff
A visit to India and a conversation with Dilnawaz and Aban Bana 128
Oliviera Todorovic
Sergei Prokofieff in Belgrade 131
Van James
A Recollection of Sergei Prokofieff 132
Barbara Mraz
Companionship in Life 134
Fabio Montelatici
Life Encounters 147
Gerard Hermans
Meetings in Holland 149
Simon Blaxland-de Lange
Some Reflections of a Translator 151
Roger Pauli
Memories of my Friend Sergei 154

Diana Pauli
Some Notes about Sergei's Contributions to the Class Lessons 156
A more personal memory 157
Carina Vaca Zeller
Impressions of a Friendship 158
Rebecca McGrath
Impressions of Sergei Prokofieff 162
Ulrich Oelssner
Building with Sergei Prokofieff 164
Christiane and Martin Wigand
Sergei Prokofieff in South Africa 165
Thomas O'Keefe
In Memory of My Life-Encounter with Sergei O. Prokofieff 166
Ursula Heusser
Sergei Prokofieff and Eurythmy 176

BONS MOTS AND ANECDOTES
Charlotte Blume
Thoughts grow together 179
Konstanze Volbehr
Displeased 179
Robert Veitenthal
Competence and Intellectual Assurance 179
Stefania Bergamini
When abroad 180
Helga Fehling
Presence of mind in everyday circumstances 180
Hans Hasler
Together 181
Manfred Heid
A good piece of advice: humour 182
Günther Herrmann and Ursula Oermann
Visit to Allgäu 183
Martina Hiemer
Koktebel 183
Wolfram Graf
Sergei Prokofieff's voice 184

Peggy Elliott
Sergei's secretary 184
Diana and Ruth Pauli
Some amusing stories 185
Ingrid Mochner
Russian 186

About the Contributors 189

Foreword

This booklet of memories of Sergei O. Prokofieff, which is here made available to English-speaking readers thanks to the deep interest of Sevak Gulbekian from Temple Lodge Publishing and the heart-warming engagement of Simon Blaxland-de Lange as translator, is intended to present a kaleidoscope of personal encounters and descriptions from various periods of his life, so that some less-known sides of this widely known lecturer and profound author of anthroposophical books may be illumined by different people.

The impulse for such a book came originally from Dr Virginia Sease, who on New Year's Eve 2020 urged Hans Hasler and me to assemble the voices of people with whom Sergei was on intimate terms, especially those older than he was. It was also important for Virginia Sease to tailor her own contribution especially for this English edition. A first collection of such memories initiated by Peter Selg and me already in 2017 could find some expression in the short contributions and anecdotes. The accounts of Sergei's childhood and youth in Moscow deriving from members of his family circle give many-faceted insights into the surroundings that so strongly moulded his personality; and these are followed by brief descriptions of the anthroposophical activities in the Russian underground and of his remarkable journey to Western Europe from October 1981 until March 1982. There are also contributions relating to this time in Dornach and his membership of the Vorstand at the Goetheanum. Friends whom Sergei met in the course of his journeys further afield report of meetings in countries such as New Zealand, Chile, India, Hawaii and England and reflect his further life's path as an active anthroposophist. To some of these people, Sergei granted deep insights into his being, his way of working and the nature of his research and revealed the love of humour, warm-heartedness and sensitivity which were combined within his essentially solitary nature.

Since Sergei's death, some of his closest friends have unfortunately also died; their contributions are therefore missing. I want nevertheless to thank with all my heart those friends who have courageously found the words to express what was living within them from their encounters with Sergei. The many notes make the music colourful, and each voice finds its characteristic tone. Many facts which would otherwise have been forgotten shine in a new light. It is a beginning which is necessarily incomplete and random in its scope; and it also cannot be regarded as a carefully considered and critical biographical study of the remarkable individual in question.

I should like to thank our dear friends at Temple Lodge for all their work of editing and proofreading, and I wish them the very best for their future endeavours.

A book has arisen from the work within the Sergei O. Prokofieff Archive, in cooperation with Hans Hasler as co-editor, which would seek to enable Sergei's personality to speak to his friends in a different way. May it find a warm-hearted interest!

Astrid Prokofieff, 3 February 2025

AUTOBIOGRAPHICAL

Sergei O. Prokofieff

33 Years as an Anthroposophical Author: an Overview

In 2014 Sergei O. Prokofieff himself published a brochure listing all his books and additionally wrote the present brief biography and an introduction to his work and its aims.

Brief Biography

1954	Born in Moscow. Studied painting and the history of art at the Academy of Arts in Moscow.
1968	Encounter with anthroposophy in the home of Maximilian Voloshin in Koktebel, Crimea.
1973	First connection with underground anthroposophical work, initially in St Petersburg and three years later in Moscow. Since then, intensive involvement with anthroposophy, with a particular focus on Christology and the anthroposophical path of schooling as the path to Christ for present-day humanity.
1976	After first hearing the Foundation Stone Meditation in German, independent learning of the German language through reading Rudolf Steiner's lectures.
1976-77	Collaboration in performances of the first and second Mystery Plays as an actor and a scenery painter in Moscow (in the underground).
March 1977	Member of the General Anthroposophical Society and since the end of 1979 a member of the First Class of the School of Spiritual Science.
At Christmas 1979	Lectures on the Christmas Conference in Moscow. A request from a member of the group for a written transcript led in 1980–81 to the writing of the book *Rudolf Steiner and*

	the Founding of the New Mysteries (published in German in 1982, in English in 1986 and in Russian in 1992).
1973-1985	Twelve years of active anthroposophical work in the underground during the time of Soviet rulership.
1981/82	First visit to Dornach. Lecture in the great hall of the Goetheanum. Lectures in London, Dornach and Stuttgart.
1985	Move to Switzerland, three years later to Germany. Beginning of a worldwide lecturing activity of altogether 2,268 lectures in four languages (Russian, German, English and French). All lectures were given completely freely and without notes. In this way, what Rudolf Steiner conveys in one of his lectures (20 July 1924, GA 240) as a task specified by Michael was taken seriously, and therefore the giving of lectures was always more important than the writing of books. 27 conferences were held in Europe alone about the esoteric foundations of the Christmas Conference.
March 1989	Asked by Jϕrgen Smit to become a Class Holder for Russia and Ukraine, and shortly afterwards for the area of Bad Boll/Eckwälden.
At Christmas 1990	Co-founder of the Anthroposophical Society in Russia. Headquarters in Moscow with centres in St Petersburg and Odessa (festive inauguration in summer 1991). Country representative until 2001.
1991	Collaboration with the conference of the School of Spiritual Science in Järna (Sweden), where for the first time all nineteen Class Lessons were given in free renderings.
2001	Appointed as a member of the Vorstand (Executive Council) of the General Anthroposophical Society at the Goetheanum. Move to Dornach.
2011	Cycle of ten lectures to mark the 150th birthday of Rudolf Steiner in the Goetheanum about his biography from an esoteric perspective.
2012	Lecture in the great hall of the Goetheanum on Rudolf Steiner's death-day, 30 March 2012.
2013	Retirement from the Vorstand for health reasons. In the following time, the main focus was on writing.

A Perspective of the Future of the Anthroposophical Society and the Goetheanum

When I was appointed in 2001 as a member of the Vorstand of the General Anthroposophical Society at the Goetheanum and of the leadership group of the School of Spiritual Science, I agreed mainly in order to work intensively also in this context on the five anthroposophical themes that had been my principal fields of activity hitherto; for they appeared to me then, appear to me now—and will above all continue to do so in the future—to belong inseparably to the Goetheanum, in so far as it would seek to develop further in the sense that Rudolf Steiner had hoped in order that it may indeed become a place of the new mysteries. These themes are:

- Nurturing the relationship to Rudolf Steiner.
- Intensively studying the content of anthroposophy and above all anthroposophical Christology.
- Cultivating an ever better understanding of the Christmas Conference of 1923/24 as the foundation of the new mysteries.
- Developing the esoteric aspect of the Anthroposophical Society (often erroneously confused with the esotericism of the First Class); for the founding of the General Anthroposophical Society was an esoteric act of the highest order. At the Christmas Conference, Rudolf Steiner had created a special organ for the nurturing of this particular esotericism of the Society and the mutual exchange of its members, namely *What is happening in the Anthroposophical Society? Members' News-sheet*.
- Strengthening the effectiveness of the First Class of the School of Spiritual Science through cognitive work and the further development of the General Anthroposophical Section as a place of spiritual research.

With the beginning of my activity in the Vorstand, I had hoped to cultivate these five themes further and to such a degree that they could begin to radiate forth from there into the anthroposophical world and thus endow the worldwide community of anthroposophists with orientation, encouragement and enthusiasm. And from the world-encompassing network of anthroposophical branches and groups of the School of Spiritual Science, a further development of these themes could potentially stream back to the centre in Dornach in order to support and enliven it and inspire it towards ever further work in this direction.

However, after ten years of service on the Vorstand I have to say that I was unable to attain this goal. I did not even succeed in establishing some rudimentary steps towards it at the Goetheanum in a manner that could be sustained. Likewise, the attempt that I made in the second year of my work on the Vorstand to establish a Christological Section at the Goetheanum did not receive a positive response. The manifold interests at this place are going today in different directions. Moreover, during my ten years in the collegium of the School of Spiritual Science there has been no general conversation about the anthroposophical and School-related themes contained in my books. Nevertheless, my conviction remains that only the fulfilment of this fivefold task can enable the Anthroposophical Society, the School of Spiritual Science and the Goetheanum, as their focal point, to become what the spiritual world expects of them in the sense of the Time-spirit.

Not only my Vorstand activities but already my first anthroposophical book and the greater part of my lectures and publications in all these years were devoted to this endeavour. I therefore have firm confidence that the aims that I have outlined here will eventually be attained also at the Goetheanum in the future; and I hope that on the path to their fulfilment my written works will have a deepening and supportive influence for all who have aspirations in this direction.

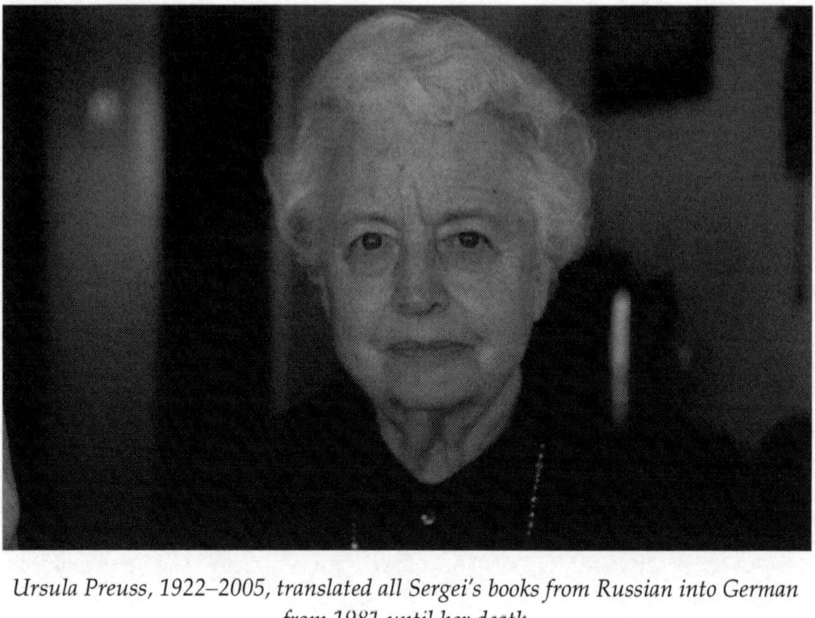

Ursula Preuss, 1922–2005, translated all Sergei's books from Russian into German from 1981 until her death

CHILDHOOD AND FAMILY

Sophia Leonidovna Prokofieva

Seryozha's Childhood and Youth

Sophia Prokofieva at her dacha near Abramtsevo, c. 1984

It was a cold, snowy winter. By all accounts I should have given birth by 31 December, at the very end of 1953. But the time went by, the birth was delayed. It was already 1954 according to the old calendar. I waited patiently, immersed in a kind of aloof but, nevertheless, blissful oblivion.

Initially, the labour pains began. I don't remember who took me to the birth clinic—my husband Oleg or my father. It was the regional nursing home named after Nadyezhda Krupskaya. The portrait of this stern lady in the waiting room greeted all the already fearful mothers with a haughty, judgemental look. It was as though her cold countenance was saying: until the revolution has encompassed the whole world there are things that are more important than bringing another human being into this world. I awaited the midwife Rosa Ruvimovna, who was to facilitate the birth of my baby. But she was not there. Time passed.

It was a difficult birth, since the child was already quite big. Sergei came into the world in the morning twilight of 16 January 1954. Someone's voice called out with a sense of relief: 'It's a little boy, and how big he is!' When I looked up, I saw a little child in the arms of Rosa Ruvimovna, who slapped him on the back. Then there was a general cry of celebration; while a strange, unfamiliar and remarkably thin voice resounded deeply within it.

Seryozha was brought to me only on the third day. He was completely swaddled, only his face was visible. He slept soundly. He was a very pretty baby. His face was as though chiselled out of rose-coloured porcelain, rightly and perfectly formed. Suddenly he awoke, looked past me to somewhere above. He had big, light-grey eyes, but with a quite particular pale-lilac tinge. 'This is the happiest day of my life,' I thought for some reason. Nevertheless, I still think so now.

At last we were discharged and returned home. But to our consternation, the little boy cried unceasingly. In the evening we summoned the doctor. Seryozha's collar-bone was broken. But this was not the reason for his tears. The doctor said that this happens with new-borns, but it quickly passes. However, he was crying because he had an infection of the middle ear. The doctor prescribed penicillin injections. Leonid Evgenyevich, my father, always gave the injections. After a few days the ears ceased to be painful, and the endless crying stopped.

Seryozha slept badly at night and had to be rocked to sleep in my arms. I remember these sleepless nights. But during the day he slept sweetly and peacefully with his arms over his head. Maria Ivanovna, my mother, sat for a long time by his bed, even though she was by then already seriously ill. She leaned over the bed and every time said with tenderness: 'My dear little Baltic baron!' When I subsequently told Seryozha about this when he had grown up, he was somehow astonished. 'How could Granny have known about this? For it is after all so.'

As a child, Seryozha most closely resembled his father Oleg. He had a fair complexion, his eyes radiated inner light, his hair was of a light-brown colour. I had little milk. We found a wet-nurse. She was a pretty young woman who had enough milk for her little daughter and also for Seryozha.

I did not want to call him Sergei. The combination of Sergei and Prokofiev had become too familiar, and I suggested the name Dmitri. Oleg laughed: Dmitri Prokofiev and Sergei Shostakovich!

Seryozha was quick to stand, and soon his pattering of feet could be heard throughout the house. One couldn't take one's eyes off him for a minute. He ran about indiscriminately, bumped into chairs while clutching hold of the carpet. He was constantly covered with scratches and bruises, but hardly ever cried. My father sawed off all the corners from tables and chests of drawers, removing the sharp edges and sometimes softening them with pieces of cloth.

No new toy interested him for long. Cars were left without wheels, board-games remained in their bright-coloured boxes.

Oleg was not a caring father, although he loved Seryozha in his own way. When Seryozha was three years old, I separated from Oleg. We tried not to traumatize Seryozha and did all we could to prevent this. Seryozha regularly visited his father, made excursions with him at weekends and was able to share many interests with him until in 1978 Oleg emigrated to England.

The two cousins Sergei Olegovich and Sergei Svyatoslavovich

Seryozha was growing ever bigger, but he was always easily excitable and disturbed. Samuel Evgenyevich Feinberg, my beloved uncle, in a sense my second father and also a great pianist, had very little contact with Seryozha. 'I am too old, Sonechhka,[1] he exhausts me. Please take him back with you!', was his constant request. I could understand him. He had already suffered one heart attack, and wherever Seryozha was there would always be noise, bustle and running about. Something would fall and get broken. He could indiscriminately press the keys of the piano, which was particularly tormenting for a musician's absolute ear. Uncle Senya[2] was especially worried about his great quantity of medicines, which Seryzha could easily reach. They were kept in drawers or simply on the night-table. Among them were little glass tubes enclosed with stoppers. These contained very small tablets of nitroglycerine, which were as tempting as little sweets. It was easy for the boy to have fun pouring them out and swallow them. This could have been fatal for the child. Uncle Senya and I decided to wean Seryozha from this dangerous game with medicines. 'Do you want to try the medicines? But they have a nasty taste!' said Uncle Senya. 'I do! Give me some!' said Seryozha cheerfully, anticipating some fun. 'Well, then'—and Uncle Senya handed him a quinine tablet. Seryozha put the pill in his mouth and chewed it. The expression of his face changed in not the slightest way. He stood there looking intently at Uncle Senya. 'Give me some more!', he said grimly. Uncle Senya handed him another tablet. Seryozha took it, and suddenly his face was distorted with pain. He cried desperately, rushed to me and put his arms around me. I led him into the kitchen, gave him some sweet tea and a bar of chocolate. But he spat it all out again. Finally, he calmed down. 'Mummy, why did Uncle Senya want to poison me?' After that, Seryozha did not touch Uncle Senya's medicines.

Seryozha coped with my separation from Oleg more easily than I might have expected. This became possible because my new husband Victor quickly came to love my complicated and unusual boy with all his heart. Victor started engaging him in a number of absorbing pursuits. They began carving wooden chess figures from smooth pieces of wood with a little penknife. For as long as they were working on pawns, everything seemingly went well. But when Seryozha tried to

---

[1]Pet name for Sophia.

[2]Pet name for Samuil.

carve a knight, he came to grief. The knight remained headless, and Seryozha parted from it by showering it with his bitter tears. I still carefully keep these pawns in a wooden casket.

Then Victor made a remote-controlled car for Seryozha. Of course, it was far from perfection in all its details. At the time such remote-controlled cars did not even exist abroad. The car moved from where it was, went to the right and to the left and then stopped. It was a kind of strange miracle ahead of its time reaching towards us from the future… But after playing with it for a short while, Seryozha became despondent. 'A bad car,' he said angrily. 'There's nothing to attach the cord to. How am I to make it go?' 'It drives itself!', I tried to convince him. 'There's no interest in that!', he said resentfully.

The friendship between Seryozha and his stepfather deepened month by month. Victor was not only endlessly patient with him, he simply loved him dearly. In a letter that he wrote to me, Victor indicated: 'I have not so much a fatherly but a maternal feeling for the boy.' Seryozha began to call him Daddy. But Victor prohibited this: 'You have a real father, Oleg. You are his son. And for me you are my dear boy. Call me Victor. This will be the grown-up thing to say.' This closeness always remained.

When Seryozha was five years old, I placed him in a private child-group. 'What a pretty boy! How beautifully he smiles! He will like it here!'—this was how Seryozha was greeted on the first day. But after a short time the tone of our conversations changed dramatically. The teacher's eyes became cold, there were no more smiles. 'A difficult child. Cannot make contact, troubled, restless.' I had hoped that Seryozha would somehow settle and get used to the situation, but suddenly a real catastrophe ensued. It so happened that Seryozha was interested in a heavy magnet in the form of a horseshoe. He observed how the magnet attracted metal. One day he was so stirred by this that he began to swing it to and fro. And then something irretrievable happened. As he swung it, he inadvertently struck a boy a year older than himself, the son of a famous violinist, on the head. The boy cried, and blood poured from his head. The scandal was deafening. That very day my son was dismissed from this elite group.

Yes, Seryozha was to blame for the accident. As we walked home I reproached him. 'How could you be so careless?' Seryozha sullenly confirmed: 'It was an accident, I didn't do it on purpose.' I soon managed to place him in a small group of only five children very close by on a neighbouring street. The house was small and fairytale-like, resembling an old tower. Over the door there was a window with coloured panes, and behind the hedge there were a few trees in a small garden. But here everything finished even quicker. On the third day I was asked to take the 'dreadful' child away.

I was then glad that I could take my five-year-old son to a group for truant children that was near at hand, in our Miussky Park. The group was led by an elderly lady by name of Rahel Solomonovna. Her grey hair came out from under her little grey cap, her face was also grey; and her eyes radiated a similar pallor. But when I came to take him home and anticipated receiving the familiar portion of complaints and reproaches, I unexpectedly heard: 'What a splendid boy! What a soul! Believe me, this is a remarkable child.' The group was small. The children were peacefully pottering about in the sandpit, while Seryozha was sitting on a bench snuggling up to Rahel Solomonovna's grey blouse. It seemed that she was telling him about the whole of her difficult and simply tragic life: concentration camp in the north, rats that gnawed through the pockets of her shabby clothes in the hope of finding even a mere crumb to eat. The kindly Rahel Solomonovna often said to me: 'Don't give him expensive toys, he won't deny anyone anything, he will give away whatever is asked of him. I have already taken it away from him and hidden it in my pocket.'

One day Seryozha returned home very aroused and excited. 'Mummy, a friend came up to me. He is already grown-up. Soon he is going far away to the island to search for gold. He said that if you will let me, he will take me with him.' I cannot pretend that this did not concern me greatly. Indeed, I was really worried. 'Who was this friend?' I asked Rahel Solomonovna who the strange man was who approached Seryozha. But she had seen no one and was merely surprised. The next day Seryozha said that the friend had again approached him. He gave Seryozha a little rose-coloured shell such as one often finds in the sand beside streams. Then Seryozha became sad—the friend hadn't come for several days. 'Do you know what he is called? Does he have a name?' 'What do you want to know this for?', Seryozha asked resentfully. 'He's simply a friend, that's the main thing.' Two days later the friend brought him a piece of rusty iron. 'This is part of an anchor! You see? And you didn't believe me!', Seryozha said triumphantly.

Sergei in the zoo, where as a little boy he took great pleasure in being allowed on several occasions to ride a pony

I then became quite agitated; for whenever Seryozha and I went anywhere, it would happen that highly presentable people came up to us who introduced themselves as film producers and offered to make a film with Seryozha in which he would play the main part. After all, Seryozha was very good-looking. However, Victor and I were opposed to this and always refused. I now decided to find out more about this unusual friend and his strange visits. Near the bench where Rahel Solomonovna usually sat there was a wooden shed where spades, rakes and an old dishevelled-looking besom were kept—everything necessary for tidying up the public garden. The shed was surrounded by thickly growing bushes which never flowered, covered with dusty leaves. Squatting behind the bushes, I observed Seryozha for an hour and then another hour. He was messing about in the sandpit, carrying a bucket of water which he poured on the dry sand in the hope of building a sandcastle. When we arrived home, Seryozha sadly told me: 'Again my friend didn't come. There are things he has to do.'

This night I was unable to sleep. I was tormented by disturbing emotions. The next morning, after seeing Seryozha off, I again hid behind the bushes. This time too there was no one. Only a thin, stray dog arrived and sniffed around in the corner of the sandpit. But Rahel Solomonovna chased it away. Then at last everything became clear. In the evening Seryozha joyfully said to me: 'Today my friend again came to me. Just think, his compass is broken! What a nuisance! But he is awaiting a favourable wind.' I was greatly relieved. For several days I had been hiding in the bushes in order to be sure; and it was now clear. According to Seryozha's stories, his friend had been there, he had again come to him. My poor little dreamer! How lonely he was. The imaginary friend acquired ever new, vivid features. A dangerous and courageous friend! He made Seryozha's life more exciting and colourful.

Shortly afterwards we journeyed to our dacha. Seryozha rejoiced, as though for the first time seeing the streams flowing over the stones, the green grass on which he could run barefoot, the flowers and butterflies. In the neighbouring dacha lived Misha, a boy of the same age as Seryozha. I had very much hoped that the two would make friends once they had got to know one another. There were so many alluring games and things to do in the country! Victor caught a little hedgehog, which had come to visit us on our terrace. Seryozha fed it with cheese from his hand. But the hedgehog unexpectedly became a stumbling block hindering their friendship. Misha wanted Seryozha to give him the hedgehog. But my son, who was usually so generous with his playthings, on this occasion simply couldn't part with the hedgehog.

It was early summer. This year there was a particular invasion of all sorts of beetles at the dacha. Without fear of people, they flew low with a buzzing noise and crept over the grass. Misha liked treading on these splendid, big insects with their blue-green lustre. Their solid wings were broken with a crunch beneath his feet. One day I heard Seryozha crying sorrowfully. I ran down the steps of the terrace into the garden. Misha lay on the grass. Seryozha was standing over him with his hand upraised, holding a half-crushed beetle. 'Why have you killed it? It may perhaps have little children... You're wicked, wicked!', Seryozha was saying through his tears. 'I shall stand here over you like this for the rest of my life holding this beetle! My whole life!' After this event the friendship between the boys was totally shattered.

Schooldays

There was then the next great test: the French school on Dostoyevsky Street. How nice Seryozha looked on 1 September in his new grey uniform with a big bunch of flowers! He was excited, happy, he really looked forward to this day. The older pupils solemnly led them into the school, holding each boy by the hand. The heavy door slammed shut. With this began years of suffering both for me and for Seryozha.

After a few days the teacher of Seryozha's class, Lyudmilla Petrovna, summoned me to the school. 'In brief, he's a difficult boy. I placed him in the front row, but this doesn't help. He listens absent-mindedly, assimilates new material with difficulty, has a poor memory and is constantly distracted. Homework is done in a slipshod way. Can you do something about this?' So I began learning with him in the first class. Every day I sat at the table beside Seryozha, but nevertheless things did not improve much. The little sticks were not arranged equally, plus and minus signs were forever changing places. The right exercise-book was usually missing in his satchel. 'Another new exercise-book! Not a single one has been continued to the end!', said Lyudmilla Petrovna angrily. 'I advise you to consider whether Sergei might not learn better in a normal school. Perhaps there he might…'

Even in the most difficult Stalinist times, the students of the Moscow Conservatory were allowed to club together at New Year to give a present to their professor, Samuil Feinberg (Uncle Senya). Usually this was a set of cut-glass crystals. Over the years we had accumulated rather a lot of these. It therefore became something of a habit to transfer one of these to the cold embraces of Lyudmilla Petrovna. She received the gifts with indifference, almost reluctantly, as if to say that this was small recompense for all the complexities and problems added to her by such a restless and unpersevering pupil. But to be honest, I find it difficult to blame Lyudmilla Petrovna. Seryozha was not only bad at mastering new material but also hindered her in her lessons by speaking loudly, jumping around and dropping things. I remember the next time that I was summoned to the school. I stood with a sense of doom before Lyudmilla Petrovna expecting the deserved blow. She looked at me with a weary reproachfulness. 'Someone has to be the last pupil in the class…', her voice rang out metallically. I could hardly disagree with that. 'But the gulf between Seryozha and the worst pupil is so great, a gulf that he will never be able to bridge.' Lyudmilla Petrovna looked at me almost with pity. I returned home perplexed and distressed. 'Now then, Seryozha is a special boy,' Victor said soothingly. 'He has such a rich imagination! You will see, he will come to surprise us all!'

When later the end of his school studies approached, I went with Victor to the school-leaving ceremony. Seryozha had by now grown up and was dressed in a severely styled blue suit. The headmaster of the school congratulated him with a smile and handed him his school-leaving certificate. He had all fives, with the exception of a four for chemistry. Suddenly his first teacher, Lyudmilla Petrovna, appeared. 'But who is this? Surely not that same Seryozha Prokofiev who studied with me in the early classes? Then he hardly managed threes! This cannot be! And now he is even congratulated!' And as though bearing some kind of grudge, she disappeared into the crowd.

Koktebel

It was in the summer of 1961, shortly after the event described at the end of the section on Sergei's childhood, that Seryozha and I made the journey to Koktebel. I remember the fascinating impression that the sea made upon him. He could stand motionless for hours by the shore, looking somewhere into the distance. Of course, I took Seryozha to the House of the Poet to visit our family friend Maria Stepanovna Voloshina.

I should like at this point to say a little about the remarkable meeting of my father, Leonid Feinberg, with Maximilian Voloshin. My father was thirteen years old at the time. After a serious bout of pleurisy he was advised by doctors to journey to the south, to the sea. Friends of the family had told him about the hospitable dwelling of Max Voloshin, the famous poet. They wrote Max a letter in which they asked him to give refuge to the boy, who passionately loved to paint. This led to a long, deep friendship between poet and teacher.

Many years had passed since then. Maximilian Voloshin had long since died, and Maria Stepanovna, the poet's widow, gave hospitality to all who had bonds of friendship with her late husband. This was for her a holy task. Because of Max Voloshin's friendly relationship with my father, I therefore became a regular guest in the House of the Poet. I was on intimate terms with Maria Stepanovna and simply called her Marusya.

And now Seryozha and I were in Koktebel. We ascended the steps leading to a wooden terrace. I asked Marusya to show Seryozha the library and Maximilian Alexandrovich's studio. I sat on the terrace drinking tea from Marusya's slightly cracked mug, and I was surprised that they were taking so long. Finally, they returned. I looked at Seryozha and hardly recognized him. He was pale, pressed his lips together and sternly frowned. Marusya wearily sat beside me. 'Well, did you like the studio?', I asked. Seryozha did not even look at me. 'Marusya!', he said with a serious, grown-up voice. 'When you die, leave all this to me.' 'Seryozha!', I cried, 'How can you say such a thing!' But Marusya stretched out her hand to me with the palm extended, as though warding me off. 'Sonya, listen to me,' she said firmly. 'This is my boy. You shall return to Moscow, just go! Leave Seryozha with me until the end of August. My friends will travel on the train with him and keep him company. And you will meet him in Moscow.'

I left, but I continued to be concerned. I secretly feared that Marusya was taking on too great a task. And so it proved.

Not far from the House of the Poet was the dacha of the well-known writer Marietta Shaginyan. She had a grandson, also called Seryozha, who was a year older than mine. Both boys considered Marusya to be their property, and each one believed himself to be her favourite. When the little jealous boys met, they fiercely seized hold of one another and rolled about on the floor, knocking over chairs and breaking Marusya's cups. They drove Marusya to the point that she went into the sea as if to drown herself. This made such an impression on the boys that their wild fights ceased.

My Seryozha continued to be Marusya's 'little boy' right until her death. She became for him a kind of second mother. He went to see her twice a year. When he was older, he looked after her when she was ill. He read the whole of Dostoyevsky and Dickens and many other books to her aloud. Of course, Voloshin's extensive anthroposophical library, which Seryozha not only read but also studied, gave a powerful impulse for a deepening interest in anthroposophy. Furthermore, it was possible for him to have long conversations on this theme with his grandfather, Leonid Evgenyevich, who was also an anthroposophist. In accordance with Marusya's legally attested will, Seryozha was to inherit Maximilian Voloshin's golden cross, which he wore next to his skin. Unfortunately, this did not happen.

Sergei with Marusya, Maria Stepanovna Voloshina, c. 1974

Again we shall return to Seryozha's early years. When he was seven years old, Seryozha acquired a little sister, my daughter Mashenka. Mashenka was weak. She suffered from diathesis, and the little girl hardly slept at all at night. Victor and I took it in turns to cradle and rock her. Naturally, all the family cares were concentrated on the frail, sickly newborn girl. At this time I received a letter that Maria Stepanova had sent from Koktebel. 'Dear Sonya! A baby has just appeared for you. Things are probably difficult for you just now. If you want, send Seryozha to me. We also have a school here. Consider my suggestion. Kisses, Marusya.'

I went to Victor with this letter. 'Look, what a strange letter from Marusya! I've only just placed Seryozha in a French-orientated school. And what does she mean by saying that a baby has just appeared? Should Seryozha go to Koktebel in the winter? This is completely absurd!' Two years later I went to Koktebel. I reminded Marusya of her strange letter. Without saying a word, she pulled out a drawer of the old writing-desk and held out a piece of paper on which was written in block letters: 'Marusya, a baby has just appeared. No one needs me here. Take me to stay with you! Seryozha.' The little rascal! Of course he could feel done out of his fair share of our care and attention. Everything was focussed on the sickly, often whimpering little girl. But gradually everything became normalized, and Seryozha again felt the attention that he had had formerly; and he stopped being jealous.

It was soon after this that my father began telling him the legend of Parsifal. Seryozha was deeply impressed, enthused and enchanted. He sat quietly and peacefully on a little bench which had been roughly fashioned in the village. Seryozha could listen for hours to this great legend cuddling up to his grandfather. King Arthur and Guinevere, Tristan and Isolde, Lancelot—they all took hold of his imagination but became not merely occasional guests but made a lasting impression on his soul.

Some years later he was admitted to hospital with appendicitis. The ward was big, with eleven children. In the evenings Seryozha told them his beloved legend. When the time came to take him home, the children broke out in tears. 'Please don't take Seryozha away! Leave him here for a little while longer! He hasn't finished telling us the story, he's at the most interesting place…' Subsequently he began to write a play called 'Parsifal', but he didn't finish it.

In 1963 Victor brought his eldest daughter Zhyenechka to see us. She was eight years older than Seryozha and was of the same mould as Victor, with a nobility and wholeness in her nature. It took some time for me to embrace her as my own, and it was not easy.

When Seryozha became bigger, we went fishing every summer for a month. On each occasion Victor led us to a new unfrequented place in the northern wilderness. We especially loved Karelia. Both Zhyenechka and Seryozha took great delight in these journeys and enjoyed packing rucksacks for them. We usually camped in tents. But once we had the good fortune to have the use of a big barn full of fresh hay. The barn was on the outskirts of a village and right on the bank of a stream. Although Victor led us to the wildest places, we were always provided with fish. We slept on the soft hay having spread out our tents. High above us there was a massive wooden beam which supported the roof. Swallows had built a series of nests and hatched their nestlings. During the night they were fairly quiet, every now and then flying off and then returning to their place. One of them, evidently a young and inexperienced swallow, was the first to let the fledglings leave the nests. One and then another fell from the nest directly onto Zhyenechka. It was the time of the white nights. And every time a fledgling fell, Zhyenechka—tall, thin and in her long white nightdress—stood up, took Seryozha in her arms and tried to lift him as high as possible; and Seryozha, holding the fallen fledgling in his hand, put it back in the nest.

The years went by. Seryozha grew up. When he went into the fifth class, where the subjects were taught by different teachers, he began to learn more easily. He already read fluently in French. He continued as before to spend much time with my father. They shut themselves in his grandfather's room and had long discussions about all sorts of things and read a variety of books.

When Seryozha entered the seventh class, the three of us—I, Seryozha and little Mashenka—journeyed to Saulkrasti by the Baltic Sea. One day Seryozha came into my room looking strangely serious and troubled. 'Mummy, I must say something to you. And it is very serious. I have... changed. I am changing my handwriting. I don't like my former handwriting. Now everything will be different, you will see!' Indeed, it seemed that Seryozha had indeed changed. One could have thought that he had grown up several years at once. He was now a calm, focussed and somewhat reserved boy. I still have one of his school exercise-books. One half is written in a formless, illegible hand, where the letters are of totally different sizes and go in different directions. The second half of the exercise-book is written in a calligraphically refined style. Since then and to the end of his life he wrote even short letters or notes in this way, as if he had never written otherwise.

When we returned to Moscow, Seryozha said that he wanted to learn German, probably in order to read the works of the founder of anthroposophy, Dr Rudolf Steiner, in the original language. I bought Seryozha some German text-books and suggested that I invite someone to teach him at home. Seryozha looked through the text-books and said: 'Mummy, that is not what I need. Look, here is a kitchen: a table, a chair, frying-pans, saucepans. And here is a tram-stop: carriage, passengers, passers-by... These words are of no use to me. I want to begin reading Goethe's *Faust*.' 'But that is very difficult,' I protested. 'Only those who know German really well can read *Faust*.' 'I shall begin patiently with a dictionary.' I remember that in the first days Seryozha read one or at best two pages of this great work by Goethe.

I left him free. A short time passed; and I saw with astonishment that Seryozha had already read the second part of *Faust*. It turned out that by this time he had already mastered the German language. Subsequently, he also learnt English independently.

Seryozha as Poet and Painter

But let us return to the early period of Seryozha's childhood. When he was seven years old (it was probably after a journey to Koktebel), he started writing his poems in block letters. I am endlessly grateful to my stepmother, Vera Nikolayevna Markova, the second wife of my father Leonid Feinberg, for having carefully collected these separate pieces of paper and transcribed Seryozha's poems in a note-book. We were struck by the gloomy mood of these poems, which was uncharacteristic of a child:

> The knight fell from the horse,
> His soul flew away,
> And his warriors died.
> And his wife died.
> And his places were broken up,
> Where he lived, where he slept,
> Where he played in the morning
> On his grandmother's knees,
> Where he gazed from the window
> At the expanses of his homeland,
> At the young forests
> And the grasslands of the steppe.
> In the night the people came
> And set up a stretcher,
> And left bloody stains.
> They bore him to the grave,
> They laid him in the grave,
> Filled it with earth
> And went away with the dawn.

And here is a poem written when he was eight:

> A man is walking in the rain.
> And an umbrella protects him from it.

He rejoices with his song.
His enjoyment will soon cease
And grief will be his undoing.
The rain has already washed away the traces.
Without father and mother he will continue his path.

For the ten years that Seryozha spent at school, he hardly wrote any poems. Only at the age of seventeen did he again return to poetry. Over the course of three years he wrote more than four hundred poems. He wrote them exclusively at night. It was as though they were already ready to be written down and caused him to awake. After writing a poem, he lay down again and went to sleep. I am unable to understand why he did not say anything about them even to his grandfather, with whom he was spiritually very close. After three productive years he abandoned poetry and even appeared to forget about his poems. Much later after several decades he chanced to rediscover them in the depths of his bookcase. The discovery came about in the following way. Those responsible for the Sergei Sergeyevich Prokofiev Museum turned to us with the question whether we had any of the composer's personal effects. It happened that in our home we had an old bookcase that had belonged to Sergei Sergeyevich. We also found his old wooden coffee-grinder. When clearing out the bookcase, my Seryozha unexpectedly found a whole pile of odd pieces of paper. On each of these were one or two poems. Here are two poems from these great cycles.

Seryozha wrote very often about death in his poems, but almost always in connection with the theme of resurrection.

In brittle equilibrium I embraced the law.
All transitions, all movements of the Spirit.
And a quiet voice, a barely audible cry
Brought its tidings to my inner ear.

In the Cosmic Will did I immerse myself,
Lent wings by Powers not of earthly hue—
It seemed to me that at the abyss I stand:
And I fall, that then I may be saved.

When Seryozha was seventeen years old, he wrote a poem which he dedicated to me. But I read it several decades later when he found it in the bookcase. It impressed me with its profundity and tragic anticipatory perspective of the future.

Dedicated to S. P.
A word is simple—like a stone.
A stone—a fragment of the sea.
A thought... who can measure in advance
Joys and grief's degree?

Forgive me that I cannot now return,
Your sorrow and your sad abandoned glance
Oppress me. And your face so dear to me
Veils reproach for what I have forsook.

But so it was—you know not how with fate
It's difficult to argue. The way is far.
I must be crucified! And grief will follow,
But do not cry—my time has not yet come.

Thus feeling's mystery I've failed to hide,
Although in deepest silence did'st preserve it.
All is now to see—not burn away,
Although the parting will indeed be cruel.

Lightly have you borne the maternal cross.
That earthly debt... dreams cannot be averted.
ETERNITY has touched you, too, unseeing—
And I matured from such quiet words as these.

The sunset was abrupt. We all became
Severe, weighed down. The world became deserted.
And in our home no more meet we with songs—
Inwardly you did not wish for this.

But may both days and destinies pass by.
An immensity will meet us at this threshold.
The world has there its refuge that awaits us:
Storm winds are stilled—just TENDERNESS remains.

At this time, Seryozha was unexpectedly drawn to painting. He greatly liked the still-lifes painted by his grandfather Leonid Evgenyevich Feinberg. To begin with, Seryozha painted plaster heads with charcoal and pencil, but that was only a preparation. When Leonid left Moscow for longer periods, he began to paint still-lifes in watercolours and oils according to the technique of the old masters in dark colours with a glaze. Only when Leonid was not at home did he continue to paint his still-lifes. He did not want to be influenced by him and wished to preserve his own style. Beginning from 1972 he studied at the Strogonov School for Arts and Crafts in Moscow and in 1977 graduated from there in the field of monumental and decorative art.

I was struck by the mastery and completeness of his first pictures. One might have supposed that he had undergone a long period of intellectual instruction. It was the sure hand of a professional artist. He had an excellent feeling for colour, shading and composition. A few years later he gave up painting for ever and never returned to it. One of his early still-lifes is hanging in my room, and I continue to appreciate it for its perfection and originality.

I shall now cast my inner eye over Seryozha's destiny. After writing over four hundred poems in the course of three years, he abandoned poetry. He was then nineteen years old. Only after four decades did he in 2012 write one further last short cycle of poems, 'Five Epistles to a Rose'. A strange, unexplainable event inspired him to write these. In December 2012 a beautiful dark-red rose grew up and blossomed beneath his window. It was overwhelmed by the onset of winter and was frozen by the snow and ice.

I often ask myself why my son, who was so gifted both in painting and in poetry, nevertheless abandoned the realm of art and chose a different destiny for himself. I now understand that the world of his spirit was so filled and saturated with anthroposophy that he no longer had the need to express his deep and beautiful feelings in any other way.

In Switzerland, probably during one of my visits to Dornach when—many years after Victor's death—I was staying with my daughter in a hotel room in Basel on the banks of the Rhine, Seryozha in a mood of heightened spirits related something strange to me. He was walking beside the Rhine and suddenly heard behind him the unmistakable, firm steps of Victor. He looked round and saw only people whom he didn't know. Suddenly, Seryozha heard a uniquely familiar voice that he could not confuse with anyone else's: 'Seryozha, you are doing everything right.' This was a unique, inexplicable event in his life. Seryozha was not inclined towards mystical visions or strange supernatural fantasies; but it was important for him to share with me this experience and his trust in an existence after death.

How does childhood come to an end? Can one delineate a clear threshold when one relinquishes one's illusory hopes and dreams? No, childhood passes away gradually, quietly and imperceptibly when one's consciousness has already accumulated new inner forces. I knew that Seryozha had a difficult path of deep spiritual endeavour before him that his soul had chosen. But I knew that he would withstand it, that he was ready for the path that he had chosen.

Addition in accordance with what Sophia Leonidovna related in a telephone conversation on 26 October 2022, annotated by Astrid Prokofieff

After his painting studies at university, Sergei was obliged to undertake military service—a frequently difficult period of life not without its dangers and characterized by coarseness and teasing. Through the mediation of an influential friend of the family it became possible to dispatch him to a unit where he was able to serve for two years in the military theatre and later also in the military orchestra and choir of General Alexandrov, who achieved fame through artistic performances.

The theatre required extras, stage hands and scenery painters, and recruits were detailed for these duties. Nevertheless, the tall, thin young man with the melancholy face did not fit very well with the desirable picture of prospective soldiers and creative members of the proletariat. There was an occasion when a scene was being rehearsed, and to make up for a shortage of actors two soldiers were summoned—Sergei and a comrade: 'You are, after all, patriots, so play your part well!'; and both had to try to pretend to be a traitor. It turned out that Sergei's comrade was chosen and, greatly to his relief, not Sergei himself.

He was then transferred to the General's library, since it was presumed that, as the grandson of the composer, he could write and read music. Sergei had to organize the whole library—literature and music—which he managed very successfully. He was, together with a colleague who was also the son of a composer, installed as a copyist in order to write the parts of individual instruments for the orchestra's performances and to distribute them on the desks for the rehearsals and performances. He also had to be responsible for the cloakroom and guided tours through the theatre for performances for children, which he did with skill and pleasure.

During this time of being quartered in barracks, Sergei intensively learnt foreign languages in his spare time. This was harmless. In the second year he was to the joy of his mother and family permitted to live at home, especially as this was only a short walking-distance away. Sophia observed that she never saw her son in uniform. It was extremely unpleasant for him to wear such clothes.

'House of the Composers', Ulitsa Chayanova 10, where the Prokofiev family lived

Valentina Chemberdzhi

Seryozha in the Circle of his Family

It was during a warm autumn day in Moscow that someone rang our doorbell. On the threshold I saw in the light of the sun a couple who at first sight made a strong impression on me. This picture was inscribed in my consciousness like a still from an old film: an exquisitely dressed lady with black curls and dark, fiery eyes and sharply formed features; and a young man, Seryozha, leaning on her with a youthful smile. There was something aristocratic about his appearance; he had an unusual, incomparable beauty of the northern Russian type, with his golden hair and blue eyes. He was somewhat taller than the lady who accompanied him and who was evidently his grandmother. The word 'grandmother' was out of favour. Seryozha called Lina Ivanovna by the Catalonian term 'Avia'—she came from a Catalonian family.

I sensed an atmosphere of boundless love and trust that reigned in 'Avia's' relationship with her grandson. It was perhaps Lina Ivanovna's trust in Seryozha that was one of the circumstances that enabled Sergei to sustain his precipitous path to the end and to become one of the leaders of the world anthroposophical movement, and from 2001 one of the six members of the Executive Council (Vorstand) of the Society at the Goetheanum, Switzerland.

Lina Ivanovna Prokofieva and her grandson Sergei Olegovich Prokofieff through a quite particular set of 'state' circumstances lived together with us in the same house, in the first 'House of the Composers' in Moscow that Stalin granted to the Moscow composers in 1937; and although it is strange to say this, a sense of friendship prevailed in this house. My mother and father were among the first inhabitants of this house, as was likewise Seryozha's family, which consisted of representatives of almost all the arts: the legendary pianist, Professor of the Moscow Conservatory Samuil Evgenyevich Feinberg, his brother Leonid Evgenyevich Feinberg, an outstanding artist who was fascinating in his ceremonial habits; the charming Sophia Leonidovna Prokofieva, a talented poetess and the author of much-admired children's books; Sergei Prokofiev's son Oleg, a constructivist artist; and later the regal second wife of Leonid Evgenyevich whose gifts were outstanding even in this circle, Vera Nikolayevna

Markova, a philologist, the author of highly sensitive translations from Japanese, a scholar of classical Japanese literature and a divinely favoured poet. The spirit of these gifts filled every wafting of the wind in the big, five-bedroom house where they lived without impinging on one another: the open grand piano, music ready to sound forth at any moment, the enormous brightly coloured portrait of Leonid Evgenyevich's first wife, Maria Ivanovna, Sophia's poems which won everyone's hearts... and in the midst of all this was Prince Seryozha. Any of the musicians, artists or poets could have taken him under their wings. This honour fell to Leonid Evgenyevich, who with youthful enthusiasm gradually and without pressure immersed Seryozha in the world of spiritual values.

At the foundation of the world-conception of both grandfather and grandson there lay Christianity, which found in Seryozha a zealous servant but did not, however, satisfy his passionate search for truth.

Sergei in 1963 aged nine with his maternal grandfather, Leonid Evgenyevich Feinberg, 1896–1980

Under the influence of Leonid Evgenyevich he was led step by step to anthroposophy; and this became the substance and content of his whole life.

The young years of Leonid Evgenyevich passed through a difficult, hungry and exceptionally awful time of executions, wars and a bloody dance of interchanging authorities, years of which we people of the twentieth and twenty-first centuries know with horror and despair only from books, reminiscences, letters and other testimonies left by those who lived at that time. One revolution followed another; the tsar was murdered together with the whole of his family. Disorder, the absence of institutions of any kind, reigned in the whole of life, in the army, in former state establishments; and queues of hungry people stretched for miles. Nevertheless, art repeatedly proved its capacity to exist and even flourish in what appeared to be the most unthinkable conditions.

A portion of the Russian population abandoned the country, but among the remaining poor and hungry people filled with a thirst for change and with hopes there blossomed wondrous flower-like gifts of a poetic and musical nature; theatres thronged with spectators, the most complicated subjects called forth the answering enthusiasm of the public. Mandelshtam, Byeli, Akhmatova, Gumilyov and Blok were among the many heroes of the Silver Age at the time of the emergence of the Bolshevik government. But people held fast to the longing to create and to live artistically.

Leonid Evgenyevich entered into the innermost circle of the friends of Maximilian Voloshin, the followers of the philosopher Rudolf Steiner who believed in his conception of the world. After Voloshin had heard him lecturing in his youth, he continued throughout his life to be in an inner dialogue with him, and anthroposophy, or in Steiner's words the 'science of the spirit', became the uniting centre of the circle around Max Voloshin.

I often think of this family of remarkable people, so different in their vocations and talents, who were possessed with the fulfilment of deeds of the highest and most audacious nature while also seeking to appease hunger by making what they said accessible to those who came to see or listen to them. I am grateful to destiny that I was able to live in a real and yet unforced way together with them; I am grateful for their trust, for the books and poems of Vera Markova formed like Japanese miniatures, for the fugues of Bach performed by Samuil Evgenyevich, the poems and fairy tales of Sophia Prokofieva.

I think that the reader can easily imagine what a miracle it was in Seryozha's destiny that against all expectations, through fortune and misfortune, he was from childhood and to the end of his life able to have access to this special atmosphere of art. Nothing prevented him from taking from life everything that had been sent to him by God.

Leonid Evgenyevich played all the roles in Seryozha's life with which nature endowed him in a single figure: father, friend, spiritual adviser, mentor, connoisseur of painting, music and poetry, tireless travelling companion, benevolent magician.

From his youth, Leonid Evgenyevich spent his summers in Koktebel, in the hospitable home of his hostess, Maria Stepanovna, whose doors were widely open for all the friends of the poet and artist Maximilian Voloshin, who was revered by all who appreciated not only his art but also his true generosity of soul, which was open to everything beautiful and whose friendship became a truly priceless gift for all his numerous friends. Max Voloshin was their talisman. Seryozha often stayed with Maria Stepanovna as her guest; he knew the poems of Voloshin, Byeli and Tsvetayeva by heart and deeply immersed himself in the world of anthroposophy in her house.

Meanwhile, Seryozha's artistic gifts were well appreciated in his family, and at the prescribed time he began studying at the Academy of Arts in Moscow, where—as everyone thought—he was laying the foundations for his future profession as a visual artist. His studies were fulfilling, as could hardly have been otherwise under the guidance of Leonid Evgenyevich and with the enthusiastic support of his mother, Sophia Leonidovna. And yet…

We became acquainted when Seryozha was 17 and I was 35, on that glorious, warm autumn day of which I have written. When I look back, I would say that a friendship formed between us that was not that of a youth and an adult woman but was as though we were of a similar age. Relationships formed without any tension; everyone had known the others for a sufficiently long time, and as fellow dwellers in the same house we saw one another frequently and the subjects for conversation were inexhaustible. It was a blessing that we were all involved in something; each person was fully engaged with his or her own affairs. I remember that Leonid Evgenyevich summoned us to look at the portrait of his late wife Maria Ivanovna, and I stood as though enchanted before the great canvas on which was portrayed a beautiful woman dressed in a gown trimmed with lace in the Bryullov style which was striking in its richness and its traditional colours—I immediately thought that this portrait had come to us from a past era. From the next room we could hear Bach's preludes and fugues, while in the study Vera Nikolayevna was reading her poems of genius. And a breath of eternity was blowing.

Seryozha and I spent long evenings sharing impressions, forever interrupting one another. We were unable to stop. But suddenly… As in a film, everything disappeared; I cannot now recall why, how and when everything changed. Life necessarily proceeds along its various paths, upsets and magical moments are in constant alternation, and you only rarely find yourself in an open clearing or country road… I cannot remember when we next met. It must have been after no less than a few years.

In my memory I see standing before me an emaciated young man with sunken eyes that had lost their blue colour, with a thinness that aroused concerns about his health… My God! Is this Seryozha? Equipped with his anthroposophical knowledge, he would today have explained everything to me scientifically or mystically, but at this moment I was simply speechless. The answer was simple. Seryozha was learning German! German? Why?... He was already mastering English. All the answers that I received astonished me… The dream that burned within Seryozha bore witness to the serious nature of his intentions. Rudolf Steiner, Waldorf, Dornach, Switzerland, philosophical studies—these had become the purpose of his life. This deep thirst for knowledge that drives outstanding personalities is by no means a superficial interest. What was it necessary to do in order to bring to realization this dream that long appeared to me to be a castle in the air? Again, the answer was the German language, in order to appear at the Goetheanum in readiness to give a lecture before a learned circle of Steinerites in pure German. And this in the times of Brezhnev, when one couldn't travel anywhere and would never receive permission, to say nothing of the necessary visas… Such words as these were like another world to us. And where and with whom should one study in order to speak properly in German? And where would the books come from, and when would there be the time to read and translate them?...

But I had to take my hat off—above all to Seryozha and then to 'Avia', who immediately appreciated the position of her beloved grandson and obtained for him the necessary books, historical works, religious and theosophical tracts, and also indicated the path to where in the USSR it was possible secretly and in the underground thoroughly to learn this by no means simple German language. She led him to the circles of the most eminent professors and devoted followers of Steiner and provided him with the money to do what he needed. Oleg, Seryozha's father, was still in Moscow. He had no understanding or feeling for his son's predicament. We did not understand and never asked about the reasons that had led to the cooling of the relationship between father and son. The only suggestion that we ventured to make was that Oleg disapproved of the path chosen by Seryozha. Oleg had by this time spent quite some time in India, and this may have confirmed his fatherly disapproval of the manner of life and world-conception of his son. I write of this only in order to emphasize the significance of Avia's participation.

At the time I knew nothing of all this, other than that Seryozha was in some distant region involving himself with something complicated and inaccessible. But when I met him again after a few years, I could compare my strong impression with that feeling of admiration that Seryozha evoked on the first occasion of our acquaintance for his remarkable moral purity and his hostility to triviality and falsehood. He had changed, and there were moments when it was possible to catch traces of humour, flashes of youthful energy.

Once, in the course of ardent conversations about matters that were entirely new to me, about the meaning of life, about the power of the spirit and its decisive part in human life, about meditations and mysteries, we were speaking about the Bible, and I asked Seryozha about a certain temporal discrepancy in the Bible concerning the birth of Jesus Christ. At that time, Seryozha in his honesty said: 'There are questions that the Bible does not answer.'

We spoke about literature and discussed one of the books that Seryozha had read (I believe that the discussion was about Melville's novel *Moby Dick*), and suddenly Seryozha unexpectedly said: 'Why do we always speak about various things, but never about what is *most important*?' I was astonished. We knew one another so well—and, so it seemed to me, every step that we took—that I couldn't imagine

Sergei aged about 17

what he was talking about. The question sounded with such intensity that I have remembered it ever since. When I came to ask him what he meant, he was not put out but clearly manifested an unwillingness to continue this conversation. Thus I did not receive an answer from Seryozha, but life provided me with one some years later. The reason lay in our limited system of views or, perhaps, the untrodden nature of this territory of higher forces, of God, of the fundamental questions of faith, and of meanings that cluster round from every side.

The three of us (Seryozha, my husband Mark and I) usually sat together in our room in Ulitsa Miusskaya. Seryozha, with his bass voice, initiated us like a preacher into all manner of problems of Christian doctrine, and we, to whom these questions were relatively obscure, argued with him until we were hoarse as a means of defending our point of view. For us this was a journey into the unknown. I was helped by my knowledge of the Bible in translation, my philosophical researches in comparing Latin and ancient Greek texts; and Mark had his mathematical mode of thinking. All this led us into far distances, our conversations lasted for a long time; and at a certain point I finally came to see that Seryozha was initiating us; he was enriching our narrow world and acquainting us with fundamental problems of humanity.

The debates lasted not less than two hours, but when Seryozha left Mark and I clearly felt that we were breathing purified, fresh air, just as when after a storm all the surrounding space is saturated with ozone and the air takes on an unfamiliar quality.

Seryozha's aim, which had seemed to me to be completely unrealistic, gradually came to manifest itself. In what he said about Steiner the word 'Goetheanum' sounded forth.

Rudolf Steiner was the architect and builder of the first and second Goetheanums (the first was burnt down), the world centre of the anthroposophical movement in Dornach. Dornach is a picturesque village near Basel, where nature has always preserved a modest, ineffable beauty. Nothing here betokened anything unexpected, but suddenly there arose before us a mighty and at the same time sculpturally alive building with remarkable forms. It rises above the green hills like a cosmic ship of an extraterrestrial civilization. In 1938 the Goetheanum became the scene of the premiere of the anthroposophical version of *Faust* by Goethe, whom Steiner idolized. In Dornach Rudolf Steiner incarnated his vision and dream of an architectural image of the universe.

The life of the spirit, of consciousness, of knowledge that was opened up to Seryozha in Dornach led him to profound changes in his life; for secrets of the earthly and super-earthly existence of humanity were revealed to him in their unfathomable depths even to the heights of the anthroposophical Olympus shining in the whole fullness of Steiner's ideas, which united what had been sundered and opened up secret and open paths to self-knowledge.

In the meantime the Goetheanum has gradually been surrounded by cosy cottages appropriate to a variety of soul-moods in which the followers and devotees of the ideas of their teacher, Rudolf Steiner, have begun to meet and lead their full lives of good deeds and good ideas. Destiny led Seryozha to them, and the blue-eyed young man had been transformed into a scholar of world renown.

Something had happened, and the truth finally started to dawn on us: in all the years when we did not see one another, Seryozha was living as our neighbour spurred on by his goal (doubtless with the ardent and steadfast support of Leonid Evgenyevich and Vera Nikolayevna) of becoming a Steinerian, a philosopher and anthroposophist. All those years he was by day and by night learning German, for he wanted to feel himself to belong in the full sense to this environment; what mattered was to learn German both for communication and for the writing of historical, philosophical, ethical and psychological works and also for life at the Goetheanum in Switzerland, visiting it on his journeys and imparting anthroposophical teachings. I frequently had occasion to hear the most admiring reports of Seryozha's lectures and presentations throughout the world. If one returns to his youth, one could say that at the foundation of all his frantic efforts was one thing in particular—imparting the word of God to the faithful; and he achieved his goal and mastered the German language. This was the secret of the extraordinary success of his first lectures at the Goetheanum, when he won the hearts of all the listeners with his inner ardour, his beauty, his language and his deep penetration of anthroposophical ideas.

When Sergei was no longer with us, I mentioned my friendship with Sergei Prokofieff in a conversation with my doctor, an adherent of the medical discoveries of Rudolf Steiner, in this case of mistletoe therapy. He was silent for a long time and regarded me with different eyes, wholly unable to believe that I was so closely acquainted with the great (*sic!*) Sergei Prokofieff, not the great composer but his grandson.

It should not remain unmentioned that Seryozha revered his grandfather and his music. In our conversations in Moscow we often spoke about music; we never missed concerts where Prokofiev's music was being played, we had arguments where we compared Prokofiev's music with that of Shostakovich; and I once noted down an emotional speech of Seryozha's which I found particularly interesting, unexpected and also revelatory of a certain aspect of anthroposophy. Here follows a short excerpt of what Seryozha said which I published in my book about Lina Prokofieva.[3]

> Sergei Sergeyevich—the composer—had a particular capacity to distance himself from all unpleasant things, and indeed this relationship to life forms an essential aspect of his work. In this sense I see a principal difference between the creative work of Sergei Sergeyevich and Dmitri Dmitriyevich Shostakovich. All those horrors that Shostakovich observed around him he at once transferred to his music, which

[3]Valentina Chemberdshi's biography of Lina Prokofieva appeared in Russian and Spanish: Valentina Chemberdshi, *XX vyek Lini Prokofievoi*, Moscow 2008; Valentina Chemberdshi, *Una española en el gulag*, Barcelona 2009.

> possesses such a tragic sombreness and an immense power of influence. Prokofiev was a person of a different order. His work studio was for him a kind of temple, and once he had entered it and began to work he left everything that disturbed, pained or even tormented him in the everyday world, including success and fame and political problems, on the threshold. In my view, Sergei Sergeyevich is the last composer in the twentieth century who is fully healthy in his soul. In the darkest periods of his life, when he was close to despair and had come to recognize the tragic consequences of his return to Russia, he continued to write pure, radiant and life-affirming music. And he did this not in order to please the political situation but in a far higher sense—in the sense of the calling of every great artist to bring to people tidings of the spirit, as one who overcomes the inertness of matter and the imperfection of life and of man. For him music was a heavenly art; and he saw his task as one of bringing it to the world in such an enlightening and uplifting form that it can bear tidings of inner strength and creative joy, qualities that in his opinion are inherent in every human being.

Meanwhile, life for Seryozha was very hard: his aims were high and far-reaching, and Russia did not give him the least possibility openly to serve his beliefs and his understanding of the world; and all his activities, whether they concerned meetings with like-minded people, his zealous studies of the German language and his approach to the status of a native speaker, or philosophy, theosophy or anthroposophy, had to happen in secret, in the underground. He overcame all impediments of the regime and, to the joy and pride of his grandmother, made it to the Goetheanum in 1981. In February 1982 she was, as a worthy head of the family, present at Sergei's wedding in Edinburgh.

In 1985 he was after long efforts able to travel from Russia. Life in Switzerland and later in Germany opened up all possibilities, and work became a constant source of inspiration. Since he was now wholly immersed in giving lectures, writing books and articles, he allowed himself only rarely to devote his time to travelling with Avia. She followed Seryozha's life attentively and accompanied him.

Since Lina Prokofieva had after her release from the Gulag in 1956 settled first in Moscow, then from 1974 in Paris and later in London and our family had moved to Spain, whereas Seryozha and Astrid lived in

Sergei with his grandmother Lina Prokofieva, the first wife of the composer Sergei Sergeyevich Prokofiev

Switzerland from 1985 onwards, we continued to meet only rarely. But the telephone conversations were endless. They were happy times for us all.

I remember that in this same period I had a certain feeling that Seryozha was as before full of unexpressed ideas and plans. Our conversations in various countries were by no means frequent, but we sometimes saw one another several days in succession. This was, for example, the case in Berlin, where we met with Katya (she is my daughter, and is almost the same age as Seryozha) when she was moving house. Seryozha helped enthusiastically with the move. This was a happy encounter which was not burdened by anything, but I remember that I discerned some kind of mystery in Seryozha's mood. Certain phrases that he uttered rang out like taut strings. My intuition did not mislead me and after some time when already in Spain we received a beautiful book published with an impeccable taste—the volume of Sergei Prokofieff's poems.[4]

The book is furnished with an Introduction by Sophia Prokofieva. I should like to quote the whole of it here, but I shall venture to cite at least a few lines:

---

[4]Sergei O. Prokofieff, *Misticheski ogon' dushi. Yunoshyeskiye stikhi* ('The Mystic Fire of the Soul. Youthful Poems'), Novoye tisyatelyetiye, Moscow 2013.

> I now know that he wrote the poems mostly at night. It was as though they woke him up and came to him virtually in a finished state, as a gift from above. I do not know anything in all literature to compare with it. I was astonished by their spiritual power and mystical depth. It is difficult to imagine how such a youthful consciousness could contain such a wealth and intensity of mystical experiences... I am grateful to destiny that at the end of my life's journey I was able to read these poems, and that the astonishing inner world of this young soul, which is without comparison, has been revealed to me.[5]

As I hold this collection of Seryozha's poems in my hands, I am gripped by the thought of how one young man was able to write so many such poems that ring as the taut strings of a soul filled with an ardent faith. I am left with the feeling of unbelievable purity and strength; but whereas the first part or even three quarters of the book is full of a tragic attitude from which a salvation can be found only in God, in His wisdom and infinite forgiveness, fortunately towards the end the poet's mood is blessed with a certain enlightenment.

The troubles came later. Why did an ailment lie in wait for Seryozha like a pitiless assassin? We were crushed and overwhelmed, and we grieve even to this day. It happened that at this very time I was afflicted with a nasty illness. I write of this in order to say that in those days we often spoke with Seryozha on the telephone; he spoke of the future in a voice that was somewhat subdued in comparison with his former bass tones, but without any trace of complaint or vexation. But I shall never forget how he once said to me: 'You and I are living now in another world.' I was struck by these words. He got to the root of it and knew that there would be no mercy for him. In this period of my illness I sometimes felt that loneliness 'in another world' of which Seryozha spoke. In that conversation long ago about religion we were discussing something entirely different, but the fact that it was somewhere decided that Seryozha, a holy servant of the good, was to be taken from us was unforgivable. Now seven years have passed without him, but he is indeed with us, living and beautiful, embodying the divine hypostasis of the human spirit.

---

[5]Ibid., p. 5–6.

Every day I look for a long time at the photograph that stands on the bookshelf opposite the sofa, where the young, dazzlingly beautiful Seryozha in the bloom of his youth is inclined towards Lina, and they are cheerfully talking about something or other.

Barcelona, 2021

Katya Chemberdzhi

Memories of Childhood

I actually have few memories of Sergei, but what has remained was very important to me as a child and in my youth. It was not that we saw one another regularly, for our lives were very different. This was not a decisive factor in our relationship. What mattered for more was that Sergei was an utterly faithful friend. This friendship was a kind of constancy in my life.

We became acquainted with one another quite early on; I do not any longer know how and when. It was most probably by chance. I was twelve years old, he was six years older. The first impression was very strong. We lived in the same house, but with access to various entrances.

Our house had a large courtyard or playground. At that time there were no children's playgrounds. Our playground was centrally placed and was connected to two other open spaces. The areas on the left and right seemed to me to be frequented by gangs, where groups of children often had fights.

I recall that when we first met we walked in a circle around the central and the left spaces and simply conversed. We spoke about Greek philosophy, astronomy and other natural sciences. I was at the time very interested in these things and still am today. I remember that I encountered a lack of understanding with my fellow pupils; they regarded me as crazy. I had another wonderful friend, Sasha Natsakanov. With him I played other interesting games. I was generally considered to be not quite normal, but Sergei accepted me as I was. He not only supported me but told me a lot of interesting things. They had to do with philosophy. I had a very thick book about the history of philosophy which I was reading at this time, and we had many arguments, or to be more precise had intense discussions. The seriousness of these debates and their profound interest impressed me.

There was never a shadow of romance in our relationship. This does not happen very often; it was far rather a true friendship. This is still important to me now, even though it unfortunately lives only in my soul and in my memory.

There was a time when we saw one another fairly often, since we lived in the same house. His thoughts and his manner interested me. He was rich in ideals, cultured, serious and knew much. I was fascinated by what he had to say. But the fact that he was interested in me was astonishing. I recall certain memories, for example when I made a house from chairs in the middle of the room. I loved building a tent with chairs and covers and making it cosy inside with a lantern and books. Sergei liked to sit in it, although he was probably twice as tall as I was and didn't fit so well. I obtained, for example, an electric device with which I was able to switch on circuits in a series of light bulbs and little bells. Sergei supported me in these diversions and said that I was doing it well, because I was very precise. Then we had my father's boxing gloves at home and we even tried to train. The fact that a girl was standing before him did not trouble Sergei. He took it all seriously and never fooled about. Everything was serious, upright and respectful. Respect for other people was an outstanding characteristic of Sergei. I cannot remember situations with him where he did not show respect. Great respect for people, seriousness, uprightness, honesty without bigotry and kindness were qualities that he always manifested. Of course I did not reflect about this at the time, but when I think back to our friendship then these feelings are again enlivened.

Sergei taught me many practical things, for example how to clean paint brushes. I always do it like this whenever I paint something. I take a piece of soap and wash the paint brush with it. This may perhaps interest no one, but for me it was a great discovery. Moreover, Sergei asked his stepfather, Victor, to put his telescope on our balcony. I can recall my mood—I always wanted to become an astronomer—when we observed the moon together and it turned out to be round. This was something that I knew, but to see it with my own eyes was something quite different. The clouds moved past the moon, and the closer they came the faster they seemed to go.

I now have four telescopes in the house. Unfortunately I cannot use them, because on the one side there are too many trees and on the other too much light. Nevertheless they are there and remind me of that telescope of Victor which, thanks to Sergei, stood for a long time on our balcony. This is one of my early memories, when I was 12 or 13. This telescope that Victor built accompanied Sergei and stands in his house in Dornach.

Then I remember that Sergei and I learnt English. We had the same wonderful teacher whom we greatly loved. I can also recall that I went to see Sergei at home. My memories of his home are only vague, but what made an overwhelming impression on me was the strong presence of art—paintings, sculptures, books and a grand piano. All these beautiful works of art barely left open a passageway to the kitchen. They were the life content of the inhabitants who had made or created them. I even remembered the blow pipe that Sergei with great care taught me to use. I knew the inhabitants of the home, but above all Sergei and his younger sister Masha, with whom I developed a friendship and had many discussions.

When we were all grown up, life changed. There was a large park near our house in Moscow. We often went for walks there. One day Sergei took the opportunity to show me a book by Rudolf Steiner. Perhaps he wanted me to become familiar with it. At some point he started speaking a lot about anthroposophy; he was very taken up with this. It was difficult for me to find some connection with this way of thinking. Subsequently, when my daughter was in class four in the Waldorf School in Berlin, I saw how significant this anthroposophical movement is. When I then visited Astrid and Sergei in Dornach, it became clear to me that it has an enormous power within it. Nevertheless, it was difficult for me then when I was younger to find a way of approaching it. I simply didn't understand it. I had a strong impression of the seriousness and dedication with which Sergei devoted himself to anthroposophy. He spoke a lot with me about the soul and its developmental phases. Much of this I understood, other aspects seemed strange to me.

Then life led us to different places: Sergei to Switzerland and me to Berlin. We saw one another only rarely, but we always had good encounters. Sergei remained an utterly faithful friend; he was genuinely, and not out of politeness, interested in what was going on, in my musical and compositional work, my family and my children, in life in Berlin, the leaving of my homeland and in much more. I recall my work on an article which was not subsequently published. I had asked Sergei's advice about it. He was the kind of friend with whom one could speak about such things and who, when interested in the matter concerned, could give serious advice that led more deeply into the subject. We spoke about Dante and the 'Divine Comedy', which fascinated me at the time, and about Botticelli's illustrations for it.

When I remarried, we visited Sergei and Astrid in their house in Dornach. It is a very beautiful house with a pleasant atmosphere created by Sergei and Astrid. I remember the enormous library, which with its array of books emanated a feeling of special happiness.

In Dornach Sergei showed us the splendid Goetheanum and told us a lot about it. I was very glad for him, for this was the place where everything came together, where his youthful immersion in anthroposophy had become his life's task. His devotion to anthroposophy, his enormous efforts, from studying the language to writing many books and giving numerous lectures, had led to everything fitting together and—to the extent that I was able to judge—he could take up a position as a member of the Executive Council of the Anthroposophical Society which is what he would have wished.

I miss the utterly faithful friend which he was. And sometimes I think of what he would have said in this or that situation, or I recall our youth and our friendship; and an answer to my questions arises within me. My memories are alive and important, and I nurture and preserve them carefully.

Elena Abramova

Meeting in New Zealand

When I was invited to perform for the artistic evening of the Anthroposophical Conference in July 2008 in Auckland, I agreed immediately and with enthusiasm. Not being a member of the Anthroposophical Society myself, I was aware of the high regard in which the arts were held by the adherents of this spiritual philosophy, and hence expected to encounter a great and very appreciative audience. I could not possibly imagine, though, that this exciting, but not unusual performance opportunity would lead to another incredible and totally unpredictable occurrence: my meeting with Sergei Prokofieff, the grandson of the great composer.

Sergei, as I discovered later, was coming to the conference from Switzerland as a guest speaker. A co-founder of the Anthroposophical Society in Russia, a member of the Executive Council of the General Anthroposophical Society at the Goetheanum, Switzerland, and the author of more than twenty books on various aspects of anthroposophy, he is one of the prominent figures in this spiritual movement in the world. Sergei's father, Oleg Prokofiev, born in 1928 in Paris, was the second son of the composer and his first wife Lina (Carolina Codina). He studied art at the Moscow School of Art, later became well-known as a painter and sculptor, and emigrated to England, where he passed away in 1998. Sergei's mother, Sofia Korovina (Prokofieva), was Oleg's first wife. Widely known in Russia as a writer for children, she still lives in Moscow.

I was astonished when I realized that Sergei was soon coming to New Zealand: not only was I working on my chapter about Prokofiev's Violin Sonata at the time, but I also, by some unbelievable coincidence, chose to play the second movement from this sonata for the conference. A probability of playing music written by one of the greatest composers of the twentieth century in front of his grandson and a likelihood of meeting Sergei personally was so overwhelming that, after firstly expressing my wish to the concert organiser to meet Sergei, I then decided for myself not to proceed with the interview, with the cowardly rationale that he would be too busy at the conference to meet me. Also, despite all my efforts, I could not think of any reasonable questions to ask—general questions sounded too tediously primitive, while personal questions could come out insensitively and intrusively. I finally came to peace assuring myself that the interview will not go ahead since I did not follow up my initial inquiry. I was thrown out of my comfortable and disgraceful retreat at once when I answered the phone and heard 'Sergei Prokofieff will meet you this week!'

It seemed that Sergei was carefully guarded—this impression, initially given me by the concert organiser, grew stronger when I tried to phone to arrange the meeting and learned that I should call a different number but strictly not speak to Sergei himself. 'Fair enough,' I thought, 'a person so well-known in both musical and anthroposophical worlds should have some protection from nosy people.' —I actually started to feel I was one of them.

Imagining all sorts of possible difficulties, I did as instructed. To my great surprise, however, a warm, very friendly voice immediately answered the phone in Russian, saying 'Hello, my name is Sergei. I've heard you wanted to meet me.' I could not believe talking to Sergei would be so pleasantly easy. The amazing journey of my meeting with Sergei and learning about his grandfather had started at that moment, as the first story followed right away.

'I'm not sure if I can tell you anything valuable for your research,' continued Sergei. 'Firstly, I didn't meet my grandfather, as I was born a year after his death, and secondly, even though I love his music, I've never played any musical instrument in my entire life. In fact, none of Prokofiev's children, grandchildren, and, as far as I know, great-grandchildren play instruments! And there is a family story behind it:' —I held my breath—'When Prokofiev, Lina and their two sons lived in Paris in the 1920s, the young children started to learn music. They lived in a small apartment at the time; the sound of wrong and scratchy notes travelled all over the flat and disturbed Prokofiev's composing. "Enough!"—he said soon—"In this family, I will be the only one who plays music!" These words, somehow, became a credo for the entire extended Prokofiev family,' Sergei laughed, 'just because he couldn't stand listening to scales played out of tune.' Looking forward to hearing more of the Prokofiev's family stories, I arranged to meet Sergei next day.

The place Sergei was staying was forty minutes away from my home, and it took me slightly longer to get there in the morning traffic. I realized I was six minutes late as I was approaching a tidy brick-and-tile house hidden away from the main road. A chill went up my spine as a flash of memory suddenly brought to me Prokofiev's notorious character trait empathized by his every biographer—his extraordinary time precision. 'Prokofiev was quite a pedant,' Sergei told me later,

> starting from the absolute order in his study, where every object and paper had its place, to the perfect system in his affairs, including financial matters. Interestingly, such a pedantic approach is not manifest in the character of his music! But one of the most remarkable

> qualities was Prokofiev's exactness with time. He could have somebody—sometimes, an important person—coming to meet him at a certain time, and if the person appeared as close to the appointment time as only five minutes early, Prokofiev would open the door, look at the person, then look at his own watch, say: 'Actually, we arranged to meet in five minutes!' and close the door.

Fortunately for me, I did not learn this story until later, and at the time I knocked on the door I was only hoping that Sergei did not inherit his grandfather's character, and just in case, prepared an appropriate apology.

My fears ceased to exist as soon as the door opened. Sergei—a tall, broad-shouldered man with a determined, yet friendly countenance—was standing in front of me. Neither had I noticed any resemblance between him and his grandfather's photos, nor could I believe that Sergei was fifty-four—so much energy and liveliness was in his expression. After a warm welcome, he suddenly said: 'Today is my only free day in Auckland. Would it be possible for you to take me to the seaside now while it's not raining, please? We could sit down and talk after we get back.' A few thoughts crossed my mind immediately: firstly, given driving times, it was obvious that we would not have time for a proper interview afterwards, and it meant that we would have to talk as we go; secondly, I realized that this situation might still turn out to be rewarding as I would have had a better chance to tackle some difficult questions on this car trip; finally, my hopes to get the interview recorded vanished instantly—therefore, I would have had to rely entirely on my memory! This decision facilitated my coming to terms with my academic conscience, and before too long, I was driving Sergei across the town in the direction of one of the finest Auckland beaches as he unfolded the engrossing story of the Prokofiev family.

Sergei told me that he was raised in Moscow in the family of his mother, who remarried after splitting up with Oleg Prokofiev. Sergei, apparently, spent a great deal of time in his childhood with his grandmother Lina, calling her affectionately the Catalan word for grandmother, *ävia*. As he talked about her, I realized that they must have been very fond of each other. He went on describing her: although Lina was born in Madrid, she regarded herself as Catalonian. Lina came from a very cosmopolitan-oriented family, where speaking a number of European languages was a part of everyday routine: her maternal grandfather was a Polish aristocrat in the service of the Russian state, so from him she learned Russian fluently; Lina used to communicate to her parents, both singers, in Italian; spoke French with her mother, Spanish with her father; and later, learned English at school in New York. Lina pursued a singing career herself, even though her voice was not particularly powerful. She first met Prokofiev in New York in 1918, where the family lived at that time: by chance, she found out about the forthcoming concert of a young Russian genius, and, interested in Russian culture because of her family history, decided to attend. The young people liked each other; in a few years (1923) they got married and had two sons. That was the happiest period in Lina's life: the tragedy of losing her husband and her imprisonment on a fabricated conviction came later, in the Soviet Union.

'Could you please tell me about Prokofiev's character?' I asked, as I headed up the motorway.

> Prokofiev loved to be in the centre of public attention, preferably in a scandalous way! This quality manifested in his youth, while he was studying in the St Petersburg Conservatory, and also in his later years abroad, especially in America. He relished his eccentricities: huge ego; extremely self-assured;—he was certain that he was a genius! Only very few times in his life he found himself in a state of crisis, when he asked himself: 'Am I really a genius?' But the answer had always been unambiguously positive: 'Yes, I definitely am!'

—Sergei laughed.

> Prokofiev was a very accomplished chess player: he managed to beat some of the world-renowned chess players at the time. He also was fascinated with a new invention—automobiles, and managed to get one for himself as soon as it was possible.
>
> Paradoxically, in the process of composing a new work he liked to work with musicians, predominantly young prodigies, such as Rostropovich. Then, he would ask them to play a certain passage from a new piece and give their opinion on the technical considerations. It is curious, how this kind of child's open-mindedness was in contradiction to his notorious aplomb.

As Sergei paused for a second, I asked: 'Do you know the reasons for Prokofiev's return to the Soviet Union? Biographers' explanations range from Prokofiev's assumed nostalgia (in a common Soviet version) and his political naivete, to the ambitious career expectations.'

'Well, I have my own version. Prokofiev went on a concert tour to the Soviet Union in 1927, where he was superbly received, but he figured out what was going on there very well.' I understood that Sergei was referring here to the political situation: the possibility of Prokofiev being unaware of what the Soviet system was like at the time was thus ruled out. 'But everybody in Europe in the 1930s knew that another war was coming,' continued Sergei, 'it was far too dangerous for a Russian to stay there.'

> Prokofiev faced two choices: he would either have to go to America, or to Soviet Russia. Unfortunately, he was not as well-known a composer as he would have liked to have been in America; that meant for him that in order to support his family (he already had two young children by that time) he would've had to give endless concert recitals, which certainly would've got in the way of his composition. He didn't want to repeat the fate of Rachmaninov, who later regretted bitterly that his career as a composer suffered so much because he had to spend most of his time as a concert performer. Not to mention that at the time Prokofiev already started to consider cutting down on his performances with the intention of expanding his composition. The other option was Russia, where the prospects for Prokofiev as a composer looked much brighter. He was promised the world by the Soviets if he decided to return: a privileged position, a good income as well as other benefits, and that every time he wrote a melody, it would be pulled out of his hands to be performed immediately. It was a very difficult choice to make, and his friend Miaskovsky's persuasive influence played not the least important role in it. Finally, Lina had the power to stop Prokofiev from going back to the Soviet Union should she insist that it would put their children in danger; however, she knew how important his career was for him and decided to support his decision. It was an ultimate sacrifice for her as she had no connections with Soviet Russia whatsoever. The children, by the way, who were twelve and eight at the time, also suffered from this move enormously as they had major difficulties in adjusting to the Soviet life as well as to a different linguistic environment.

Sergei went on with the story, obviously taking pleasure in clarifying the history of his family.

> At first, after Prokofiev returned to the USSR, everything went as expected: the family received an apartment in Moscow and other

fringe benefits; Prokofiev was well-respected and his compositions were widely performed. However, the Soviet scene, which was already different in the 1930s from that of 1927, began to change further as the regime matured, especially after *The Lady Macbeth of Mtsensk District* affair [1936, opera of D. Shostakovich which was criticised].'

'Did Prokofiev feel the pressures from the regime?'

There were two events which shattered Prokofiev, virtually caused the breakdown in his health and led to his premature death. The first major incident was the infamous Resolution of 1948, where Zhdanov attacked all the top Soviet composers, including Prokofiev and Shostakovich. Prokofiev managed to somewhat save face then, as he did not attend the official meeting under the pretext of a poor state of health; instead, he sent a rather ambiguous letter. The other devastating event was Lina's arrest. Prokofiev would have probably lived for another ten years if these things had not happened to him. You know, he had high blood pressure and died of a stroke—these conditions are commonly caused by stress and trauma.

'Are you aware of other instances when political pressure was exerted on Prokofiev?'

As I said, these two occasions were the major ones, which ruined the last period of his life. In 1948, Prokofiev learned that his reputation and the worldwide fame were no protection and anything could happen to him. Since then, he had lived in a state of fear, expecting to be arrested at any moment. That is why he spent most of his time in the retreat of his *dacha* in Nikolina Gora: he was simply afraid to stay too close to the official city life and professional affairs. You can gain a better insight into the dismal ambience of those years from the following fact: many professors of the Moscow Conservatoire would always carry secretly with them a lethal amount of poison for the event of their arrest. As people of honour, they feared interrogation more than death for the reason that under torture they might be forced to give false evidence against innocent people. Interrogators were instructed to obtain the necessary information by any means, and if they failed, they knew they would be the ones to replace the victims of torture. Therefore, they were under a huge pressure themselves. In the case of Meyerhold, they

> murdered him instead of giving him a chance for a trial because even making a written record of his anti-Stalin statements would bring an enormous danger to his investigators.

'Did Prokofiev regret his decision to repatriate?'

> He probably did, though he was too afraid to talk about it openly, not only in his flat in Moscow but even outside the city, in his *dacha* in Nikolina Gora. Apparently, there were some hints on this topic in his conversations with the children when they came to visit him there. They didn't come often, though: Prokofiev was quite a cold and distant father, especially since Mira, his second wife, had an aversion to seeing his sons from the first marriage. Nevertheless, when they managed to visit him, he would always suggest going outside for a walk, particularly if he wanted to talk about important matters. Living under threat, he did not feel safe talking anywhere indoors.

In the context of Sergei's statements, the allusion commonly found amongst Prokofiev's biographers to the composer's great love of the peacefulness of his countryside residence and appreciation of nature sounds ironically cynical! In light of the fact that Prokofiev had spent eighteen years enjoying the freedoms of the West combined with the facts that his second wife Mira was pro-Soviet and that Prokofiev was always mindful of being watched by the authorities, I could see that Prokofiev might have taken particular care to avoid discussion of certain topics inside the house or in the presence of Mira, but considering the sensitivity of the issue, I chose to leave the discussion of Mira's personality with Sergei for later.

'Was Prokofiev's compositional style affected by the circumstances of living in Soviet Russia?'

> Prokofiev never made compromises in his style, not even under ideological pressure. He also never lowered his standards of writing, unlike some other composers in similar circumstances. As a matter of fact, there is nothing stylistically 'Soviet' in the music of even his 'official' compositions: once the lyrics are removed, musical style evokes the European tradition! Despite living in fear for the last few years of his life, he would not allow his state of mind to come across in his music.

The core of Prokofiev's compositional aesthetics was his complete separation of the reality of everyday life from his creative sphere. For him, his music was like a temple—he would enter there, shut the gate behind him, and by doing so isolate himself and his music from the outside world. Prokofiev's 'new simplicity' was a natural outcome of his development as a composer and had nothing to do with the principal of 'socialist realism' or other ideological pressures. Despite some audacious experiments of his youth, he had always been essentially a composer-melodist. So, when he embraced a concept of 'new simplicity' in the second half of his creative life, he, so to say, was coming back to his true nature.

'Prokofiev and Shostakovich are usually seen as two leading Russian composers of Soviet period. Do you have any thoughts on the similarities and differences in their lives and works?'

The most obvious difference, of course, lies in these composers' different biographical background. Prokofiev was born in 1891: that means that his personality became fully shaped well before the 1917 Revolution took place. He left Russia soon after the Revolution and then spent many years abroad before coming back in 1936. Prokofiev, therefore, was a real European man and composer: 'Soviet' traits can neither be found in his music, nor in his character. There were, at the time, some revolutionary inclinations in his style, but 'revolutionary' not in the common 'Soviet' connotation of this word! Shostakovich, on the other hand, was born in 1906, lived all his adult life in Soviet Russia, and therefore virtually did not have a chance to experience any other way of life outside of the socialist order.

As composers, Prokofiev and Shostakovich represent contrasting poles of musical aesthetics. Prokofiev, in the detachment of his everyday existence from his art and putting the latter on a pedestal, perceived art as an eternal, objective and unchangeable entity. For Shostakovich, art epitomizes all the drama of experiences and feelings of a living individual. The difference in their creative perception could also be associated with a juxtaposition of the intellectual and emotional spheres, where Prokofiev elevates his art to the intellectual heights, while Shostakovich descends to the depths of human emotions. The external and objective world of the former exists in a different dimension from the internal and subjective world of the latter.

These two polarities of archetypal creative personality types invoke the Apollonian/Dionysian dichotomy.

Prokofiev's music is generally incredibly bright and optimistic (Apollonian); it exemplifies some kind of very healthy and positive attitude to life, though, again, not at all in a 'Soviet' way. Shostakovich's music personifies the sufferings of existence (Dionysian); it leaves the impression of him staring into the depth of an abyss, and sometimes even descending into it, especially towards the end of some of his compositions. I believe that the reason for such an enormous popularity of Shostakovich's music in the past decades all over the world lies exactly in this quality to move people's hearts through expressing the tragedy of being: listening to this music, people sensed that their ordeals have been lived through and shared by somebody else as well as themselves. However, these days—years after Soviet reality ceased to exist—Prokofiev's art in a new form increasingly gains popularity. This opinion, by the way, is shared by the Russian conductor Valery Gergiev, who contributed to the popularisation of Prokofiev in recent times.

The difference in Prokofiev's and Shostakovich's reaction to the denunciations of 1948 is very indicative of the differences in their creative individualities; their responses also determined their forthcoming consequences. Prokofiev, as I mentioned earlier, did not attend the meeting, wrote an ambiguous apology instead, and practically did not alter his compositional style. Thus, the sanctuary of his art remained intact. Soviet authorities had never forgiven Prokofiev for retaining his dignity, and therefore his reinstatement was significantly delayed. Nevertheless, despite the ill health, sorrows and other troubles of his last years, Prokofiev appeared upright and maintained a strict discipline in his lifestyle. It is feasible that a strong factor that supported him in that time was Christian Science, a *spiritual teaching* which maintained that the power of human thought can profoundly influence *human* life. Both Prokofiev and Lina had been Christian Scientists for years. I am aware that much later, after Lina was released from a prison camp, she was still practising this religion, as she used to secretly obtain some Christian Science literature which was smuggled to Soviet Russia from overseas. Prokofiev's spirit remained unbroken right until the end; but, as he banished his anguish to the periphery of his inner being, it eventually struck him back and took away his life at once.

In contrast, Shostakovich was humiliated openly on many occasions; of course, it caused enormous suffering for him. In 1948, he was compelled to apologize publicly for his compositional shortcomings. After that, authorities disgraced him even further by forcing him to take up the humiliating role of representing the Soviet Union for the Congress in the USA where he was coerced to publicly affirm external and domestic Soviet policies on music and other matters. However, his position was restored shortly and he was reinstated officially as the number one Soviet composer. The agony Shostakovich went through emotionally and spiritually over the years was imprinted in his features and his uncontrollably shaking hands. He wanted to greet me not only in his music but also in his physical condition and appearance, as if his body absorbed these appalling experiences. I had a chance to meet Shostakovich in the late 1960s and it made a very distressing impression on me. I recall his deeply terrified and miserable expression. He wanted to greet me with a handshake, but failed to do it properly because he could not manage to keep the hand steady. I still remember the feeling of holding his trembling hand in my hand. In his gaze one could still feel the whole tragedy of this great creative individuality.

'What do you think about Volkov's *Testimony?'*

Testimony, or at least *a certain* part of it, is, of course, not an authentic document. I read it some years ago and I had quite a few concerns about its accuracy. I cannot believe that Shostakovich would really say things that Volkov insinuates he did, especially concerning Shostakovich's hostility towards other composers, such as Prokofiev. You see

—Sergei smiles—

the essential difference between the author of *Testimony* and the personalities he brought into it is that such figures as Shostakovich and Prokofiev are great people, while Volkov proved himself to be rather narrow-minded. A good example, by the way, of a sensitive and complex relationship between prominent personalities is the relationship between Prokofiev and Stravinsky: despite the odds, the basis for it had always been mutual respect.

However, the political and social environment of the Soviet era as depicted in *Testimony* is correct on the whole. Therefore, *Testimony,* when it first appeared, turned out to be a document of great significance, since it countered the standard view (initially established by the Soviet officialdom and then accepted in the West) that Shostakovich had always been a devoted Communist and an enthusiastic supporter of the regime. *Testimony* opened up a different path for an historical approach to the life and times of Shostakovich.

As the conversation went by, I felt the time had come when I could touch on a very sensitive issue—Prokofiev's two marriages. I have always been fascinated by the possibility of political implications behind the composer's personal relationships, as well as sympathized with Lina's dreadful fate awaiting her in the Soviet Union and admired her strength and courage. In a few words, some time after Prokofiev, Lina and their two sons arrived in the Soviet Union, the marriage broke down and Prokofiev started a new relationship with a young Russian woman Mira (Maria-Cecilia Mendelson), whom he met in 1939. Since 1941, Prokofiev lived together with Mira, who is usually referred to as his second wife, although there have been some serious doubts about the legitimacy of this marriage on the grounds that Prokofiev had never divorced Lina officially. Lina, after the relationship collapsed, found herself to be in the terrible position of a foreigner living in the politically aggressive and increasingly xenophobic environment of the Soviet Union without friends, relatives, or employment, though Prokofiev continued to support her and their children financially. What is more, left in Moscow with two sons in her care throughout World War II, she endured enormous hardships. For a few years she tried to get permission to leave the country with her sons, but all her attempts were unsuccessful. When Prokofiev and Mira were finally able to register their marriage in January 1948 as a result of a new law, which automatically annulled marriages with foreigners, Lina lost her last source of protection—the official status as a wife of a major Soviet composer. A few weeks after their wedding, she was arrested, charged with espionage, and sentenced to twenty years of labour camps. Prokofiev couldn't help Lina. He himself was in a very vulnerable position at that time, since her arrest took place very soon after Zhdanov's attacks on composers. Prokofiev, who died in 1953 (the same day as Stalin did), never saw Lina again after her arrest. Lina survived the horrors of a camp; she was released in 1956, due to a general amnesty after Stalin's death, and came back to her life in Moscow. It was not until two decades later, however, that Lina finally found a way to return to the

West. She died at a ripe age of ninety-one in London in 1989. Lina never recognized Prokofiev's liaison with Mira as his second marriage: until the end she maintained that she was the only legal wife he ever had.

There have been speculations that Mira was not only a member of the Communist Party, but also connected to the highest authorities in Soviet Russia through her alleged uncle Lazar Kaganovich, a close friend of Stalin and the Minister of Heavy Industry.[6] In the light of this, an assumption of Prokofiev's split with Lina and subsequent relationship with Mira being driven by the authorities seems to be viable. However, this opinion has been argued (for example, by Malcolm Brown[7] or Harlow Robinson[8]) on the basis that there is no reliable evidence of Mira's relation to Kaganovich or of the political pressure on Prokofiev's personal affairs, while Prokofiev himself indicated directly and indirectly on many occasions that he was satisfied in this relationship. Interestingly, Brown's decisive point in his discussion of the legitimacy of Prokofiev's second marriage, which, he believes, shows clearly Prokofiev's own position on the matter, is based on a quotation from Prokofiev's letter to Vera Alpers written in 1944. Brown writes: 'A short quotation from Prokofiev himself will have to suffice for the present as a basis for inference concerning the reason for his break with Lina and his intent with regard to Myra Mendelson: "Great changes have also taken place in my life—I have divorced *(ya razoshelsias)* Lina Ivan(ovna), married for the second time, and am happy in the second marriage."'[9] This text, however, was translated from Russian inaccurately, and an exact translation rather puts Brown's conclusion in question than proves it. The correct translation of the Russian word *razoshelsia* is 'separated' or 'split up'; it might also refer to a divorce, but not commonly, since there is a much more precise word in Russian to indicate being divorced: *razvelsia.* It would be very surprising if a notoriously meticulous person and a brilliant writer as

---

[6]Victor Seroff, *Sergei Prokofiev—a Soviet Tragedy*, second ed. (London: Leslie Frewin, I969).P. 282.

[7]Malcolm H. Brown, 'Review: *Sergei Prokofiev. A Soviet Tragedy* by Victor Seroff,' Notes, second series 26, no. 3 (1970). P. 520.

[8]Harlow Robinson, *Sergei Prokofiev. A Biography* (New York: Viking, 1987). P. 366-7.

[9]Brown, 'Review: *Sergei Prokofiev. A Soviet Tragedy* by Victor Seroff.' P. 520.

Prokofiev was, accidentally used such an elusive definition as *razoshelsia* referring to his divorce instead of the much more accurate *razvelsia.* In other words, the exact translation of the text reads that when Prokofiev married Mira, he was only 'separated' from his wife. For a Russian reader, therefore, the ambiguity of Prokofiev's position, who seemed to intentionally remain vague about the matter, strongly comes across. Another, though less important, consideration here is that if Prokofiev, indeed, yielded to the pressure to replace his existing relationship with the new liaison with an approved Soviet citizen, he would also be expected to play by the rules of the political game and appear genuinely happy with his choice. Not to mention that nobody's letter written in the era of Stalin's dictatorship (especially for such an important figure as Prokofiev) could be expected to be delivered to its recipient unread by the authorities, since such surveillance was an open secret. Therefore, heavy reliance by Brown on such a letter is naive.

I was hoping that since Sergei was close to Lina, he would be able to shed some light on the intricacy of this subject and asked him to talk about Prokofiev's personal life. He elaborated thus:

> Lina was an incredible person: sophisticated, strong-minded, independent and so full of life. She was a real European 'Dame of a high class'. Lina sacrificed her standards of living, social life and career when she agreed to move to Soviet Russia with Prokofiev. Unlike him, she did not feel at home in Russia, could not accept Soviet values and lifestyle, and, instead of trying to find her place in the socialist society, blatantly socialized with foreigners on a regular basis. This conscious rejection of the Soviet way of life put a lot of strain on her relationship with Prokofiev, who genuinely tried his best to adjust to the new environment.
>
> Yet, the real fracture in the marriage occurred when Prokofiev met Mira Mendelson. You see, Lina loved the seaside, whereas Prokofiev loved mountains. As a result, they often spent holidays separately. On one of such vacations Prokofiev met Mira—a young and very ambitious woman who assumed some literary talent. Prokofiev and Mira started to work together on some projects: she wrote some lyrics and collaborated with him on the libretti for some of his operas; however, she turned out to be a pretty hopeless writer, and as soon as Prokofiev realized that, he discontinued the professional collaboration. In fact, he was a

brilliant writer himself and hardly needed anybody's assistance. It seems that Mira personally was very eager to steer Prokofiev away from his family, as she apparently had an ambition to get married to a celebrity! Much younger than Lina was at the time, Mira craftily manipulated the circumstances and certain tensions in Prokofiev's relationship with Lina. She managed to be in the right place in the right time to destroy the marriage. On the other hand, Mira fulfilled the role of Prokofiev's assistant, servant and later, nurse, which did, indeed, satisfy Prokofiev's need of the last years of his life. As you can gather from the account of Lina's character, she would hardly be suitable for that subservient role.

'So Prokofiev's choice was not forced by the Soviets?'

As a matter of fact, Lina was positive that the KGB was behind Mira's actions. I personally do not believe in it, but cannot exclude an indirect influence. However, this is a very grey area, indeed, as there are no facts to substantiate this opinion. Surely, the authorities supported and even encouraged Prokofiev's relationship with Mira as she was a picture-perfect Soviet citizen, and were against Lina who remained foreign to Soviet society. Mira was a *pionerka* and *komsomolka* [a member of Child and Youth Communist organizations] from a textbook: born two years before the Revolution, she was nurtured by the regime and did not know any other way of life.

'What happened to Lina and the boys after the marriage broke down?'

Prokofiev left in 1941, just before the outbreak of World War II. When the war started, Prokofiev and Mira got evacuated to the Caucasus, while Lina and the boys stayed behind in Moscow. Prokofiev continued to provide for them financially at all times. Lina was very reluctant to give Prokofiev a divorce, which hindered Prokofiev and Mira's marriage plans. However, when Prokofiev came to *ZAGS* [Russian Births, Deaths and Marriages] after the war, he found out that surprisingly, he didn't need to divorce officially from Lina any more since his first marriage, under the new law, was considered invalid in Soviet Russia. Thus, when Prokofiev married Mira, he ended up being married to two women at the same time! This is, probably, the only case of bigamy in world music history!

Lina, as you know, got arrested on the false accusation of espionage in 1948. She kept her associations with foreign embassies during and after the war, which was a very dangerous thing in those years. She was fifty-one at the time of the arrest; her prison term was twenty years, which meant life sentence for her. Lina maintained that Prokofiev tried to help her, however, it was a very difficult time for him, too, and his means were very limited.

Lina had an extremely difficult life in a labour camp in North Siberia. She was tortured in prison and in the camp as she appeared very alien in that environment. One of Stalin's biggest crimes, I believe, was that the political prisoners were intentionally mixed up with the criminals. That was the case with Lina, too: you can imagine how cruel it was to put somebody of her class and culture together with the common convicts. One of her struggles, for example, was that of preserving the clarity of her own speech: her inmates were determined to force her to use *mat* [a common swearing Russian jargon], which would be very humiliating for her refined nature. Somehow, Lina managed to win that battle. Luckily, Lina was partially saved from that awful environment in the last eighteen months of her camp life by a German doctor. He was sentenced, too; however, as soon as the camp authorities found out about his profession, he was ordered to serve the inmates' medical needs. The doctor, though, did not speak Russian at all and needed an interpreter. He immediately spotted Lina and requested her to be appointed as his interpreter and assistant, which included her to be living at the practice. This was an enormous relief for Lina, who now did not have to stay in the same space with criminals.

When Prokofiev died, Lina had no chance to find out about it as the prisoners had no connection with the outside world. However, that night she had an extraordinary experience: Prokofiev appeared in her dream, dressed up all in white clothes; this was a traditional picture of a dead person. Following the Catalan belief she understood that he passed away; she also construed that he felt remorseful about what he has done to her and tried to reconnect with her in this way. Only three weeks later Lina heard from another prisoner, who had an occasional access to the radio, that Prokofiev, indeed, died that day.

Lina was released in 1956, three years after Stalin's—and Prokofiev's—death, having spent eight years in the camps. At that time, Mira was deemed as Prokofiev's legal widow, while Lina was largely

> disregarded. Nevertheless, after Lina came back to Moscow, the official position towards her started to change gradually, especially after Mira's death. Gaining more and more recognition as a wife of Sergei Prokofiev, Lina received a special pension and other fringe benefits from the state. One of the new privileges was her entitlement to view any concerts and other musical events for free. Luckily, this way I also got to see the best artists of Soviet Russia and from abroad: *àvia* used to take me with her to concerts, operas and ballets. That is how I met some leading musicians of the country; one of which was Dmitri Shostakovich.

Sergei concluded.

During the course of this conversation we had taken in some of Auckland's stunning West coast and now came the time when I had to drop Sergei back. I was amazed at the fount of information he had revealed, his depth of knowledge and detailed description of the family history hugely exceeding my expectations.

EARLY YEARS OF ANTHROPOSOPHICAL WORK IN THE UNDERGROUND, 1976–1981

Pyotr Alexandrovich Chaikovsky

A Friendship since the 1970s in Moscow

We first met at the performance of the first Mystery Play in a private house in Moscow. It was the home of Pyotr Startsik. However, this first performance was without costumes and scenery, the play was read with distributed parts; and Sergei and I were in the audience. The reading was interrupted by tea breaks and discussions, through which we became more closely acquainted. But during these discussions we were still very careful; we spoke about the weather, about matters of a more trivial nature. The new ones in the group, Sergei and I, were studied closely, albeit in a friendly way, but still very apprehensively. It was, after all, still the time of the Communists, of materialism, when all religions and spiritual aspirations were prohibited and one could suffer serious persecution. Subsequently, a beginning was made with intensive studies of the works of Rudolf Steiner; we embraced anthroposophy deeply into our conversations. My impression of Sergei was not exactly one of a mature man but of someone with a wholly serious demeanour who studied anthroposophical books seriously and revered Rudolf Steiner.

The following year we performed the second play, this time with costumes and simple scenery. Sergei, Volodya Tichomirov, Vitali Kovalenko, Gennadi Bondarev, Ala Ragoshina and other fellow players were there, and we were already getting to know one another better. Whereas at the beginning Sergei seemed to me to be someone who was not wholly of this Earth, further acquaintance indicated to me that he was a person who stood clearly and firmly on his two feet and also had—quite apart from anthroposophy—a healthy faculty of judgement about the affairs of life.

In these years we began to meet regularly during the Holy Nights for festive gatherings. I can also recall the first lectures that Sergei gave about the Foundation Stone Meditation during those days, about the situation within which the meditation was sounded for the first time and about the further course of the Christmas Conference of 1923/24. He spoke with great solemnity and seriousness about the words, processes and the various aspects of the conference and the Foundation Stone Meditation. We were all young, and with a youthful enthusiasm. At some of these meetings—I do not remember when—friends from the West were also present; and I well remember Annie Jahn and Karla Kiniger, who were often there.

In these years we met in Moscow (there were approximately 12 to 15 of us) every week under difficult circumstances, every time in a different flat and in such a way that we always came alone to the meetings and never left them together, so as not to attract the attention of neighbours or the militia. Only in the bus or the metro did we meet up again. This required a very precise awareness of the situation.

There were at the time not as yet many translations of Rudolf Steiner's books and lectures. To begin with we always read the Foundation Stone Meditation in German and in Russian and we concluded with the Michael Imagination in both languages. We devoted our attention to other meditations and read what was already translated, above all the basic books and the cycles on the Gospels. The table around which we sat was adorned with either one or seven candles and beautiful minerals. Translations were made in conjunction with our study evenings, whether by Volodya or Gennadi. These were special moments.

Sergei, Vitali Kovalenko and I had met frequently. Sergei was at the time studying at the faculty for monumental and decorative art at the Academy of Arts in Moscow, then the Strogonovsky Institute in the Sokolnichesky region, where there were many art institutes at the time. Vitali and I worked not far away in a laboratory for film shots. Halfway between the two was a cafe, where we often met for lunch. Thus a small circle of friends arose that led to extensive conversations about anthroposophy, Rudolf Steiner and many other themes, not only in the anthroposophical study-evenings but also during lunch.

In August 1977 we had great plans. The Russian writer, director and actor Vasili Makarovich Shukshin,[10] who came from the Altai region, had written much about this area. He was no anthroposophist, but his conception of nature and life was very close to Goetheanism. This had awakened the interest of the three of us. Shortly after the performance of the second Mystery Play we undertook a four-week journey in the Altai region and wanted to become acquainted

---

[10]Vasili Makarovich Shukshin, 1929–1974.

Scene from the Middle Ages enacted in front of scenery painted by Sergei, 1977

with its countryside and people. The father of a good friend of Vitali, who has almost completed his medical studies, Yuri by name, lived by the Telezky lake. Yuri had suggested to Vitali and us that we go there. The journey at that time was very long: first aeroplane, then train, then for a long time in a bus on poor roads. When we got there we met an oldish man who by profession had been a hunter. He was ill, but as was often the case in those villages, he did not want to go to hospital. He knew the area very well: the healing springs, the therapeutic radioactive waters, the villages and the places of strength where special healing plants grow. One couldn't go for walks there without a knowledgeable companion. He didn't take us on hunts but was prepared to show us such special healing places on his way. These were not merely thought-out qualities but the wholly real experiences of those who lived there. He lived with his wife, who was a researcher into local history, educated as a 'scientific specialist for the culture' of this region of the Altai. She knew the old legends and songs of this area. She likewise came with us. Thus a geographical excursion resulted where we sat together in the evening by a campfire and listened to legends, stories and indications about healing plants. But every evening we also read

Sergei at the time of the Altai expedition, 1977

the Foundation Stone Meditation in Russian and German. Vitali, with his school German, was able to speak the words. Sergei knew French at the time, but he had only begun to learn German. Later he also read the meditation in German. We wandered very far; the Mongolian border was only about 25 to 30 kilometres (roughly 15–18 miles) away. Nevertheless, we decided to walk back. This was in all a quite special journey, physically very strenuous but full of new experiences of a soul and spirit nature. Our friendship deepened.

After our return the work in the anthroposophical study-group continued intensively. We together shared the themes and the reading of Rudolf Steiner's lectures and spoke about them. At the Michaelmas festival in 1979 Sergei gave lectures which subsequently led to his first book.

In the autumn of 1981 Sergei was finally able to leave the Soviet Union and visit his father in London. The journey to Germany and to Switzerland was linked with this. We were pleased for him that he had this possibility. It was clear to us all that Sergei had a special destiny and many tasks before him. We never thought that he might not come back to Moscow. He had a special mission. After his return to Moscow the work in the group developed further. In this, Sergei played an increasingly important part. He had matured inwardly. Through his very presence, a growing intensification, a festively joyful and spiritually common work unfolded before our eyes. Even later, when he was already living in the West, his presence was always a joy, like a festive day. What we beheld was a constant flow of creative work out of anthroposophy.

By 1983/84 the group had significantly changed. A split had arisen. There was a separation from Gennadi Bondarev, who formed a group of his own with his friends. In the time after Sergei's departure to Germany to be with Astrid in June 1985, the work developed further and increasing numbers of young anthroposophists joined it.

Subsequently, when Sergei was living in Dornach, I visited him several times. I experienced how seriously he dedicated himself to his tasks, worked constantly on his new books and was at the same time very taken up with conferences and lectures, while always allowing time for conversations. I visited him in his office at the Goetheanum. We had a relationship as between good friends, which is something different from being merely a relationship based on work. Thus one speaks about all sorts of things that have nothing to do with work. We also argued back and forth, spoke about the karma which arises today through all influences of civilization, about questions of the time, about narcotics, about their medical aspects and the destruction of the ego together with the subsequent karma, about the question of how the body might be formed in the next incarnation—we discussed things of this nature. Here he merely said: One can only guess how all this may be imagined.

In the autumn of 2012, Sergei Prokofieff invited Volodya Tikhomirov and me to visit the place of Tsarevich Dmitri's death in the town of Uglich. We together spent three days on a motor vessel on the way to the place of the tragic death of the Tsarevich Dmitri. Sergei was deeply interested in this fragment of Russian history and tried to carry out spiritual research in relation to it. During the journey he told us of his hypothesis. In his opinion, the Tsarevich Dmitri and the false Dmitri had the same father, and these blood relationships enabled the Tsarevich Dmitri after his death to inspire the false Dmitri for a certain time from the spiritual world. Only this can explain the fact that the false Dmitri was accepted as the real tsar. When the inspirations ceased, the false Dmitri was driven out of the country. I remember with what interest and attention Sergei examined the frescoes in the church where the history of the conspiracy and the death of Tsarevich Dmitri were portrayed! He stood for a very long time at the place where the Tsarevich died and tried with all his heart to feel the spiritual atmosphere of that time. After this journey to Uglich I had further brief meetings with him of which I shall possibly say something later.

Georgi Kavtaradze

Some Cursory Notes of Meetings with Sergei Prokofieff

The meeting with Sergei Prokofieff, which occurred in the early spring of 1976, was for me one of those moments whose significance arrests one immediately but whose understanding—and these are by no means the same thing—does not arise at once.

On that day I had without prior notice, as tended to happen when there was no telephone connection (by no means everyone had telephones at that time), gone to see Sergei Vasilyevich Zetilov, then one of the few anthroposophists of the generation in their twenties, who resided in a big old wooden house in Strelno, a settlement on the Petergofsky road that had been neglected in Soviet times. In the small room with a wood stove which he occupied, I found a young man whom I did not know sitting at a little table by the window and now imperturbably awaiting an explanantion of the situation created by the appearance of an unexpected guest. Our host introduced us to one another. I had previously heard of Sergei, the grandson of the famous composer, most likely from the same Sergei Vasilyevich. Sergei went regularly to see him from Moscow on account of cycles of Rudolf Steiner's lectures in old translations which he kept in typewritten form. (Sergei did not as yet know German at that time.) Why Sergei did not seek such a possibility in Moscow, I am unable to say to this day.

Sergei had recently passed the threshold of his fourth seven-year period; he had become acquainted with anthroposophy in Maximilian

Voloshin's library in the home of the poet's widow, Maria Stepanovna, in Koktebel in Crimea and was now intensively assimilating the rich legacy of Rudolf Steiner's lectures in translation. I, on the other hand, was approaching the recognized 'mid-point of life' and had discovered anthroposophy twelve years before, but there was in the young man whom I found at the house of Sergei Vasilyevich something that riveted one's attention to him. As I subsequently came to experience all the more distinctly, this something compelled one to accept him *for himself*, even when among anthroposophists. Before me was an anthroposophist in the flesh. One somehow tended to forget that he had not long been involved in anthroposophy. This was someone who was by no means open to just anyone's world, but it was clear that in anthroposophy he was 'at home'. It's strange that I accepted this then as something that went without saying, and in subsequent conversations with him I compared my ideas about one or another thing that I learned with what he thought about this. A restraint, a deep seriousness and a strictness defined his manner of behaviour. This was immediately obvious, but the understanding that his strictness in relations with others began with a strictness towards himself did not arise at once.

That spring I was still living under the impressions from my first journey abroad, to the then GDR [the German Democratic Republic], which was arranged for me by students from the Eastern part of Germany then belonging to the Soviet bloc (they by way of 'exchange' studied in the institute where I taught in Leningrad). It was full of impressions from my first meetings with German anthroposophists, with The Christian Community, under whose cover anthroposophists were also active in the GDR. Sergei, as though looking through me towards Germany, where he had the prospect of living, listened to my fragmentary stories about this journey with interest.

That summer I invited him to be my guest in the south, in Gagra, where I was born and where I had some rooms in a house given by my parents. Gagra is a spa town in a picturesque place on the shore of the Black Sea with remains of a Byzantine or Genoese fortress from the sixth to seventh century; square in its plan with a stone church restored at the beginning of the twentieth century within it. Portrayals of an eight-pointed 'Maltese cross' (adopted by the Maltese Order of Knights-Hospitaller many centuries later) are preserved on the stone blocks of the church. During those days that Sergei spent with me in Gagra in July, I acquainted him with what I considered worthy attention. Sergei was not drawn to the sea, but on mountain paths he climbed ever further and outstripped me.

On one of those days we went to Novy Afon [New Athos], which lies to the south of Gagra. The journey there on the electric train took an hour and a half, but I always took guests there. Orthodox monks established Novy Afon at the end of the nineteenth century, as though extending a connecting thread with the sacred mountain in Greece called Athos (in Greek, 'silence'), a stronghold of Orthodoxy in the East. As with Gagra, Novy Afon lies beside the sea. From there begins the Kolkhetis lowlands broadening out to the south. On a hill beside a river flowing from the depths of the gorge, the monks erected a big monastery, inactive in Soviet times. On the opposite bank of the river rises the peaked Iverskaya mountain with its three slopes and remains of a seventh to eighth century fortress on its summit. Down below on the side of the monastery there stands a church restored by monks from the ruins, built—according to tradition—on the place where Simon the Cainanite is buried. According to the same tradition, he was the husband at the marriage feast in Cana of Galilee, where Christ enacted the first of His miracles of turning water into wine. Simon subsequently, together with the apostle Andrew, came to these regions; and while Andrew went farther to the north Simon remained, laying the foundation for the spreading of Christianity in this part of Iveria (Georgia).

Sergei and I spent that day on the mountain dedicated to the Iverskaya Mother of God, the protector of Georgia. A zig-zag track leads to the summit of the mountain, and there we encountered a mighty fortified wall engirdled with trees. Behind it was a broad glade of trees, giving shade and coolness in the summer. We spent the whole day on this summit reaching into this airy space above. At the highest place within the fortress there are still the ruins of the ancient church with characters on the walls and a representation of the same Maltese cross which is also on the ruined walls of the church in Gagra. This is Anakopia, where, according to the testimonies of Byzantine sources, the Emperor Irakli buried his treasures in the time of the Persian wars.

The hot summer's day imperceptibly drew to an end. We decided to spend the night on the mountain. We settled for the night beneath trees with such thick foliage that we could have been shielded from the rain if any had come during the night. Before going to sleep, at

Sergei's wish I read *'Menschenseele, du lebest in den Gliedern...'* (Soul of man, you live in the limbs...). Our first sleep was broken by the cry of an owl, which was nesting somewhere above us but somehow came down close to us. Because it was unexpected I started to drive it away, but Sergei stopped me. What did the prophetic bird of Afon—'the owl that penetrates the night'—want to tell us? Or was it an eagle-owl?

In the morning we returned to Gagra, and in the afternoon I took Sergei to the other end of the town where Vitali Alexandrovich Bogolovsky, my Leningrad mentor in anthroposophy, who came for the summer to the sea from Tbilisi whence he had moved from Leningrad once he had come into a pension at the end of the 1960s, rented a little wooden house in the garden.[11] I usually called upon him during the summer. We did not normally agree on a day for the next visit. It was possible to find him at any time when he was not bathing, when he would be sitting in his little house for his regular translating work. I now wanted to introduce Sergei to him and him to Sergei. It seemed to me that these two people, despite the difference in their ages, would get on with one another. The first moment of their meeting has always remained in my memory. I could not have imagined the perturbation that Vitali Alexandrovich, who was always self-assured, manifested in that moment. He was, as it were, dislodged from his habitual rails. This was, of course, only for a moment, and Vitali Alexandrovich rapidly took hold of himself; while Sergei, as ever, maintained his self-control and did not express any relationship to the beginning of the meeting. I left the two of them together and was therefore not a witness of the conversation that transpired between them.

The following day Sergei flew to Moscow, having spent three days in Gagra. He said that it had been good for him to be there, 'only music was lacking'. When he said these words, some singing rang out to us from the street—some neighbouring Greek children were performing a popular Greek song in a choir. 'There's a bit of music, after all,' I said.

When on the next occasion I was spending my summer holiday in the south, Irakli Pardzhiani, an artist from Tbilisi and an anthropos-

[11]Incidentally, while necessarily using the Soviet name for St Petersburg, it is appropriate to mention here that Lenin's name *did not sound* in it—the emphasis fell on the last syllable which generated the meaning, while the two unstressed syllables did not cause one's attention to linger on them.

ophist who was very close to me, was staying with me as my guest. He was then under the influence of the personality of Sergei, who had been in Tbilisi not long before (this was already at the beginning of the 1980s). 'Who is he?', asked Irakli in a conversation about Sergei. This question was, of course, not addressed to me.

In subsequent years, meetings with Sergei came about during my infrequent flying visits to Moscow or his appearances in Leningrad. He was then living alone in Moscow in a flat inherited from his grandmother, and was intensely working on something. As subsequently became apparent, he was writing his first book *Rudolf Steiner and the Founding of the New Mysteries*, which—when it appeared in the German translation of Ursula Preuss—placed him in the ranks of the leading anthroposophical authors.

From the impressions of these years, which were pretty diverse in nature, there is one episode that especially deserves mention in which I was a participant together with Sergei. In March 1979 I was in Moscow for a comparatively long time—I had been officially granted a month's scientific mission which did not commit me to anything in particular. I made use of it in order to acquaint myself with the latest anthroposophical literature coming from Germany and Switzerland to the big Moscow libraries (in contrast to those in Leningrad, which did not have the golden touch to make orders from abroad). I also availed myself of the opportunity to broaden my circle of anthroposophical acquaintances in Moscow, specifically to be at meetings of friends who regularly gathered in private flats. Holy Week was approaching. Easter, which we marked by following the rhythms of the Calendar of the Soul, was awaited that year on 15 April. Sergei invited me to one of the meetings in March. As far as I remember, there were five people. It was suggested that we read one of Rudolf Steiner's lectures on an Easter theme. The intense mood of our meeting was suddenly destroyed by ringing and insistent knocks on the front door. Our hostess went to find out what was going on, but she had barely opened the door when a militiaman's cry came roaring into the flat: 'Criminals!', he yelled at those gathered in the flat, who were pretending to be brave but were nevertheless frightened. 'You've shown such resistance when I was bringing the bailiffs!' Two men in civilian clothes entered the flat behind him, people of middle age. These two forced themselves stealthily into the flat, like the rats from the governor's dream in Gogol's *The Government Inspector*, and they now looked all around them, searchingly, for traces of what had been taking place before their entrance. Our friends received the unbidden guests in a standing position. Only I continued to sit. On seeing this, the two men appeared confused—they clearly regarded me as a foreigner, but then I brought myself to speak: 'With what right are you bursting into someone else's flat?', I said, feeling that it was necessary to say something, while understanding that a question about rights was totally out of place here.

On hearing a Russian voice and understanding that they were mistaken about me, the people in civilian clothes felt themselves to be completely free and continued to rummage visually around the room. A search did not materialize. After a while they caught sight of a candle which humbly continued to burn on the low table somewhat to one side. We had forgotten to extinguish it! What is this for? This is evidence! It was probably sufficient for compiling a report about a gathering with some kind of suspicious aims. We were ordered to leave the flat and go down into the yard.

When I now look back at this scene, I recall Sergei's presence there as an afterthought—it was as though he wasn't there: he was among us and at the same time outside that situation of such drama for us. The whole of this time he stood by the wall, maintained his silence and was as though withdrawn into himself. This presence of his served as a counterweight to what was taking place which the rest of us could not create. Before we began to go down, he said to me as though recalling that I had been there not on my own initiative: 'Now we will be closer to one another.'

In the yard we were seated in militia vehicles and taken to the nearest militia department. There we were conducted through various rooms with demands for written explanations as to how and for what purposes we were gathered in the flat. When they had received our testimonies, they let us go. We parted with mixed feelings. I do not remember that we tried to evaluate what had been happening to us.

After a few days I returned to Leningrad. It could be expected that the happenings in Moscow would be conveyed on the respective channels to the attention of my institutional authorities. However, the days went by, and there was no sign that my colleagues and, what was more, the faculty leadership knew anything of what had occurred. Only a year or two afterwards, when I was forming the next scientific mission to Moscow, did the secretary of the Party organization of the faculty where I was one of the assistant professors (I should mention in brackets that, incomprehensibly, I was the only non-Party member of this 'ideological' faculty) said to me very meaningfully: 'I hope that you will be more careful to choose those with whom you associate in Moscow.'

There were still seven years until the beginning of Gorbachov's Perestroika.

Sergei's and my paths gradually went their separate ways. There are people who claim to be particularly close to him. I am not one of them. I am altogether not sure that there were people to whom he would have experienced the need to reveal himself. His wife Astrid, of course, was excluded from this restriction—this choice was one that he made for life. I recall with what delight Maria Alexandrovna Scriabina watched this couple when I once found them at her house in Moscow (this was already in 1984). But I cannot imagine that there were people of whom Sergei would have been in need. Self-assured by nature, he went through life concentrated on his own affairs. It was as though he guarded something accessible to him alone. As a faithful knight of the Sophia whom he discovered for himself in Anthroposophia—this is how I see him in those distant days.

Dieter Hornemann

Work in the Underground, as experienced by a Foreigner

It was at the beginning of November 1976 that I came to Moscow for a baptism. It was thus that I came to know of the circle around Gennadi Bondarev and Sasha Demidov. At the end of the days of my visit, it was clear that I would return. The pleas of the friends so touched my heart. When I could next be with the friends at Ascension 1977, a young art student by the name of Sergei Prokofieff had newly joined the circle. He immediately made a particularly deep impression on me: he was a sensitive, keenly discerning person. We once went for a walk together because he had some very special questions, and because in the flat there was always the worry about listening devices. Gennadi was forever being summoned by the KGB. He told them that they were an amateur dramatic circle; for they had first translated Rudolf Steiner's Mystery Plays and were now performing them. Sergei, the young art student, painted the scenery.

When I made a further visit Sergei was unable to be there; the others told me that he had meanwhile been conscripted for military service. I could not imagine him there for a moment. Then he nevertheless came to a meeting and all admired his courage for coming in civil dress; for the soldiers were—under strict threat of punishment—urged always to wear their uniform. He courageously disregarded this. Here is a brief extract from my diary, from my third journey in January 1978:

> Sunday showed itself in all its glorious array. At 10.30 Gennadi fetched me from the bookshop 'Druzhba'. We drove to Sasha's house. Sergei also came there. At midday Yura (Yuri Sennikov), the painter from Zagorsk (Sergiev Possad), Pavel, Irina and Zhenya, the first wife of Gennadi Bondarev joined us... I spoke to the three men about the significance of the year 1978. Sergei wished for a walk in order to be able to speak more in detail. The conversation was very intense, then suddenly we noticed that we couldn't find the flat. However, after further searching we did manage. Towards evening we began with my special theme on this occasion, the study of the stars. Star transparencies aroused great delight.

At the time I stuck the stars onto deep-blue transparent paper with a thicker needle so that the lamp behind them enabled the stars to be visible as in the sky. In this way we could get to know the constellations and then later find them again in the sky.

> We went outside and in the sky saw the winter hexagon, Jupiter in the Bull, Mars in the Crab and Saturn in the Lion. For all these were their first encounters. Gennadi said that completely new worlds had been opened up to him. They had long known all relations between and classifications about the stars that one can learn in anthroposophy; but it was a great revelation to them that one can also see this with one's own eyes.

In February 1982 I was to marry Sergei to Astrid Seufert in Edinburgh. They had previously visited me a few times in Stuttgart for conversations about marriage. In the autumn of 1982 I was again able to undertake a journey to Moscow, this time with my French colleague Marie-Françoise Cuvillier. I also again met Sergei, who continued to live in Moscow. Here again something from my diary:

> The mood amongst the population seemed to us to be still very oppressive. We were constantly overshadowed. When we entered a house, two markedly unobtrusive figures were standing on the opposite side who followed us equally unconspicuously when we came out again. Marie-Françoise Cuvillier spoke to the friends about celebrating the festivals with children, I studied Leonardo's *Last Supper* with them. A number of younger friends had found their way to the group. But it was not as it had been before. Gennadi had a new, very young wife; he had separated from Zhenya.
>
> During a visit to his house Sergei Prokofieff showed me his 'workplace', as he called it, a shelf with books by Rudolf Steiner from which he composed Russian anthroposophical literature through excerpts.
>
> Marie-Françoise asked me after the visit to him: Has he become a little arrogant? I said that he had to adopt a suit of armour after his time in Germany in order to be the master of all the admiration. In any event, the glorious lecture-tour through places in England, Switzerland and Germany had not only done him good. In Stuttgart he spoke in January 1982 in the assembly hall of the Uhlandshöhe Waldorf School before 1000 listeners; it was a sensation. Else Klink performed an extra eurythmy solo in his honour. Why are we anthroposophists so eager for sensations?

The constant state of watchfulness became focussed for me in a strange, very realistic dream. I was lying in bed, then the door opened. A whole number of fellows came in. One said: There he is. And a doctor in a white coat rushed at me in order to give me an injection. I woke up trembling and had to think intently of Pyotr Startsik. How dreadful it was that opponents of the regime were hidden in psychiatric institutions! This fifth journey of mine was to be my last for a long time.

I only met Sergei again from 1989, when he was already living in Germany.

Translating with Sergei

I regard the meetings with Sergei Prokofieff in Stuttgart in the time between 1989 and 1991, when we met several times at irregular intervals in order to translate the rituals of The Christian Community into Russian, as among the happiest experiences of my life. We proceeded by looking first at the translations that were already available by Lyuba Husemann, with whom I had often been enabled to act as a server during my time as a seminarist, and the one by a circle around Kurt von Wistinghausen, with which I had—together with Kurt von Wistinghausen (died 1986)—frequently celebrated in past years. I had also celebrated using this translation when a friend was present with us with his children in 1989 in the Methorst holiday camp.

Sergei undertook significant amounts of translating work alone. He thought that the existing translations resonated too strongly of the traditional diction of Russian Orthodoxy. Since he had already translated the texts of Rudolf Steiner's Lessons of the School of Spiritual Science, he had already had much experience with Rudolf Steiner's language. Günther Dellsbrügger and I essentially assisted where it concerned an understanding of the text. I would then bring the results of our endeavours to Moscow, where we had a 'trial reading' in a small circle. To them it sounded 'too anthroposophical' in many places. Their suggestions for changes were as a rule accepted by Sergei.

The work was a wonderful opportunity for us to immerse ourselves together into the depth and beauty of the rituals. The experience that we were able to have will always remain with us. I am very grateful to Sergei that he gave so much dedication and love to our Christian Community!

Peter Heusser

Memories of Journeys and Meetings with Sergei Prokofieff

During the Christmas period of 1979/80 Annie Jahn and I travelled by train to Moscow in order to spend the whole of Christmas there with the anthroposophical group around Gennadi Bondarev, Sergei Prokofieff and others. Annie Jahn from Austria had frequently gone to the Soviet Union as one of the first anthropsophists from the West, in order to get to know the Russian anthroposophists and work spiritually with them. She also spoke some Russian. She courageously also smuggled especially anthroposophical books to Russia, which was not without its risks. It was also the case on this occasion. At the Polish-Russian border, where the train had to wait for a long time because of the change to a different gauge, we were both obliged by Russian border officials to leave the train together with our heavy suitcases; our passports were taken away and our suitcases were thoroughly examined. Perhaps the officials were looking for political literature or dangerous objects, but they did not seem to be concerned about the anthroposophical books and at any rate let them through. It was only thanks to the rebellious side of Annie Jahn's nature that we managed, albeit narrowly, to get everything back into the train.

In Moscow we were, like other Westerners, accommodated in the Hotel Rossiya not far from the Kremlin, where Russian men in coats and fur hats hovered about watching and waiting in the reception lobby. Every afternoon we then travelled by the underground railway from the hotel to an outlying quarter of Moscow in order to spend the Christmas evenings festively there in Gennadi Bondarev's flat together with the anthroposophical friends. Every time that we wanted to go outside through the reception lobby of the hotel, a group of between three and four men from those waiting there separated off and followed us close on our heels to the underground, likewise got in and pursued us to where Gennadi lived. It was therefore openly demonstrated that we were being watched and that they wanted information about every step that we made. It was also not possible to shake these shadowers off. When I once tried to evade them in the throng of people, rooms, stairs and stalls in the big shopping centre 'GUM' on Red Square, I could see that I had no chance. In our absence our luggage in the hotel room was also examined, and in the middle of the night one received calls from unknown people who then hung up.

I am describing these things here in order to indicate the mood in which our Russian friends were living at that time. For they too were totally surveyed. Bondarev's home was on the first floor of one of the blocks of flats that were customary then. The friends told us that a policeman was quartered in the flat above, and in the floor and ceiling of Bondarev's flat a listening device had been installed. Several members of the group had already been questioned; and they lived constantly with the thought that at any time someone from the group could be arrested. Nevertheless, the evening Christmas celebrations always took place without restriction. By strictly focussing upon anthroposophical themes and avoiding any content that could be interpreted as being dangerous to the state, the friends there endeavoured to achieve complete transparency in the awareness that everything they did could more or less become known to the KGB. The friends told us that it signified for them a certain protection to receive visits from the West, for at that time the way that the Russian authorities were dealing with dissidents was often criticized in the West and there was clearly a general wish to avoid this. Nevertheless, the surveillance and the risks that one had to undergo were clear to everyone. When between 10 and 11 pm we again emerged from the flat and from the block of flats, our shadows from the KGB were still waiting for us in the icy cold and 'accompanied' us back to the reception-hall of the hotel.

In contrast to this dark and threatening mood, the Christmas celebrations with the Russian friends were marked by a deep intimacy, warmth and seriousness. The warm candlelight in these deep, very cold winter nights was like a real symbol for what was happening inwardly here, against the background of what could be experienced as the intimidating dark power of the Soviet state. The theme of the Christmas evenings was the Christmas Conference of 1923/24 in Dornach, and from this all-too-real historical Moscow perspective, which had at the time also a global and world-historical significance, the inner meaning of the Christmas Conference could be grasped in quite another way than what was and is the case with all the exchange of diverse, to some extent combative social and political views about this conference in the West. Especially Gennadi and Sergei gave very long lectures with which conversations were linked and which were framed by the reading of the Foundation Stone Meditation in German and Russian. As regards the content, I did not get much from them, since everything took place in Russian; and since I spoke no Russian I was dependent on receiving the occasional summary translation from Annie Jahn. All the more, however, did I let the whole mood which impressed me very strongly to work upon me.

I was at the time just thirty years old and was living in Switzerland near Kreuzlingen, whose near neighbour on the German side is Konstanz, and had made myself familiar with the history of the branch there. This branch had been established by Harriet van Vacano, who had under Rudolf Steiner's guidance collaborated in the first performance of the Mystery Plays in Munich and had in 1922—under the pseudonym of Harry Köhler—published an edition of the works of the Russian philosopher Vladimir Solovyov through the publishing house 'Der kommende Tag'. I had become interested in him and acquired a second-hand copy of this edition; I had also studied a collection of texts from Rudolf Steiner's lectures about Russia, and was fired by the significance of Russian culture for the future and by the importance of a cultural collaboration between Central and Eastern Europe and of anthroposophy for this future. This had been the main reason for my participation in this Christmas journey to Russia; after all, I did not as yet know any Russian anthroposophists. Through the freshness and broad expanses of its landscapes and through its spiritual significance (with the Irish monks in St Gallen and the influence of Paracelsus, and also with the death by burning of Jan Hus from Czechoslovakia in Konstanz), I had experienced eastern Switzerland, together with the area around Lake Constance, as a part of Switzerland with a spiritual significance for the future. On one of those Christmas evenings in Moscow, I gave a contribution about Switzer-

Work in the underground, 1977/78. Sculpting with Eva-Maria Garbe, Yuri Sennikov, Sergei and Pyotr Chaikovsky

land and its possible relationship to these future developments, for which Russia in its connection to Central Europe plays so important a part. I was the first Swiss person whom Sergei Prokofieff, who was then approaching his twenty-sixth birthday, had come to know; and we befriended one another to the extent that this was possible in those few days. He spoke a little German, so that we were also able to understand one another directly. The deep seriousness and the forcefulness with which, with his deep, powerful voice, he spoke then about the Christmas Conference, central Christological insights and Rudolf Steiner's significance for the development of the mysteries, impressed me greatly. What inner gravity and firmness came to expression from his words! And in what difficult outer circumstances all this unfolded and blossomed! It was for me a proof that future evolution depends on the courage, resolution and power with which spiritual life is grasped irrespective of the outward circumstances, and even in direct contrast to them.

I once experienced an example of this courage in Sergei when we were walking across Red Square in front of the walls of the Kremlin and he was speaking quite loudly and candidly about anthroposophy, and I caught myself anxiously looking round to see whether there were any informers in the area who might pass on what he was saying. In contrast, he was taking absolutely no notice of such people as were milling around and spoke totally freely; and this was someone who knew his Soviet surroundings much better than I did. I was inwardly ashamed of myself, in that I lived in a free country that traces its existence back to people like William Tell. For me myself, these experiences with Sergei and the whole group elicited a high degree of courage. Something else that impressed me already at that time was Sergei's stupendous knowledge of anthroposophy. He had worked as a history of art guide in a museum; and during the long periods when such a guide had little or nothing to do he had studied numerous lecture-cycles by Rudolf Steiner in German (and thereby also learning German). He evidently had an extraordinary memory, so that he was able to compose his richly content-filled lectures out of a vast perspective of spiritual themes. I was struck by this as a spiritual faculty that perhaps especially Russian people possess. In my sphere of acquaintance I at any rate knew no one of such a kind. Sergei and I also conversed about the significance of Steiner's basic philosophical writings, and I presented him with my own proof copy of *The Philosophy of Freedom* with many underlined passages, which I brought with me to study on the journey.

Thus we came to know one another at this Christmas time. I was and remain deeply grateful for this meeting. When he later came to Dornach for lectures and ultimately even, as a member of the Executive Council, to the Goetheanum, I always hoped that we could also engage in spiritual work together. Unfortunately, because of my full responsibilities as a doctor at the Lukas Clinic in Arlesheim and later at the universities of Bern and Witten/Herdecke and also through his own involvement in many duties, this never came about. We met personally only on a few occasions during this time. At the very end, not long before his death, it was still possible to share some thoughts in writing about what might have been expected from such a common work, which, however, had not been a possibility in this life but might perhaps become so in a new form in the distant future.

1981–1985: FIRST JOURNEY AND RETURN

Astrid Prokofieff

Christmas 1981 in Dornach and a Turning-Point in Life

My father, Herbert Seufert from Bonn, belonged to the discreet group of anthroposophical friends who in the 1970s visited the anthroposophical groups in Moscow and St Petersburg that worked regularly in the underground. He had met Sergei there several years before; and when Sergei came to Dornach for the Christmas conference at the Goetheanum, my father asked me to meet him and extend his greetings to him. I had come to know of these undertakings of my father only a year before. Through fortunate circumstances, I met a friend after the performance of the Paradise Play in the Goetheanum who was able to introduce the Russian gentleman to me. Thus I made Sergei's acquaintance, gave him my father's greetings and wished him a merry Christmas evening. During the following days there were many events at the Goetheanum, and I was struck by a curious phenomenon. Whenever I came to the cloakroom designed by Rex Raab and Arne Klingborg in the foyer of the Grundsteinsaal, where people approaching and going up to the room were on the move in all their different ways, I met Sergei. I now wanted to test this out and came earlier than usual. Who was making a beeline for this spot? Herr Prokofieff. Friendly greetings were exchanged. Then I ran to the Goetheanum at the last minute and hung my coat on the first hook I could find. Who was also hurrying thither with big strides? Herr Prokofieff. We laughed and went up to the hall. So it continued until the end of the conference.

Annie Jahn, who was looking after the guest, invited me to Sergei's lectures, which with the agreement of Jörgen Smit took place in the students' house late in the evening outside the conference programme. The theme 'The Foundation Stone Meditation and its Rhythms' had for a long time been worked on in the Youth Section under Jörgen Smit's leadership and was a special interest of mine. People were sitting and standing in considerable numbers in the little hall of the students' house. The modest and matter-of-fact nature of the lecture expelled the somewhat emotional mood of the older ladies. What mattered to us younger ones was the content, in which we sought insight. I was stirred by the aspect of the seven rhythms of the meditation in their relationship to the soul's path after death extending to world midnight and back again to the Earth.

His hostess was eager to acquaint him with the greatest variety of things. She asked me, as a student of the singing method of the Swedish singer Valborg Werbeck-Svardström, to introduce him to this anthroposophical work. This took place two weeks later on the festival of the guest's birthday with a singing interlude of two songs with lyre accompaniment by Alois Künstler. On the occasion of this birthday, some 30 guests who had otherwise never been together in one room had been invited to a meeting with the young Russian: representatives of the Goetheanum, Friedrich Hiebel, Hagen Biesantz, Jörgen Smit; Edwin Froböse and his wife Eva from the Rudolf Steiner *Nachlassverwaltung* (Literary Estate), Else Klink, Johannes Bleiker and his wife Carina, Elisabeth and Gerard Wagner, Eva and Raoul Ratnowsky and other friends. Sergei had met them all and they were asked to tell him of their relationship to Rudolf Steiner. With this invitation he was, therefore, bridging the barriers between streams as they had become through destiny.

Then Annie Jahn asked me during my vacation from the conservatory in Basel to undertake a walk through the neighbourhood of Dornach and Arlesheim to the Hermitage. The walk took place during a snow shower after the birthday celebration. The history of the Hermitage, which Goethe already visited, and its grottoes were the substance of our conversation, as was the legend of Parzival and my musical activities. After several hours in the wet snow, the hostess received us with some hot food and, since Sergei was now better known in the neighbourhood, he accompanied me to my house on the Hügelweg below the Goetheanum, where I was accommodated together with my piano in a tiny room in a shared flat. I was aware of a kind of brotherly/sisterly affection. Nevertheless, the following Sunday brought a surprise by the clear light of day. I was to meet Sergei Prokofieff again in the early morning, I had been informed. Sergei greeted me and pressed me for another walk, and I therefore chose Schloss Dorneck as an objective with a view of the Gempen. The conversation ended with a simple proposal of marriage from Sergei together with the indication that his visa was due to expire at the end of February and that he had to return to Russia. I gave myself three days to think about it. He had arranged further visits in Switzerland and was not reachable over the following days. I asked my parents and was glad about their spontaneous agreement, which contrasted with my anxious brother, who had shortly before read Solzhenitsyn's *Gulag Archipelago.* An inner trust in Sergei's moral integrity and the common bond with anthroposophy were the foundation for my assent, while a closer familiarity had to await the future. His two 'chosen grandmothers' Karla Kiniger from Edinburgh and Dr Ursula Preuss, the translator of his books until 2005, had long been journeying to Russia to meet with anthroposophical groups. I knew both of them fleetingly through my pedagogical studies at the Waldorf seminar. They met in Stuttgart at the end of January for questions relating to the publishing of the first book and were taken into confidence regarding the organization of a registry-office wedding. After clarifications in Germany, my home town of Bonn and England, it became clear that Edinburgh in Scotland had the most advantageous conditions for this and the time limit of the visa could be adhered to. After the lectures in Stuttgart at the end of January, a visit to my family in Bonn was arranged and necessary official papers obtained; and Sergei also gave a lecture to the branch about the anthroposophical work in Russia. It was obligatory for Sergei to tread British soil 14 days before the wedding. His plans were therefore changed, the work on the manuscript for the Verlag Freies Geistesleben in Stuttgart was speeded up. It was through the advocacy of Stefan Leber, who had come to know and appreciate Sergei in Russia in 1980, that the board of trustees of the publishers was prepared to enter into the risk of publication.

I had examinations for the end of my semester and fortunately a vacation in February. All preparations had to be made in great secrecy, since his bold 'detour' to Switzerland and to Germany was forbidden by the Soviet authorities. Moreover, his lectures were not advertised but were publicized by word of mouth without mentioning his name. The imminent publication of his first book was likewise highly risky politically, especially because—out of an inner truthfulness and responsibility for the content—he wanted to publish it under his own name.

It was a real wedding festival in the circle of the assembled families: from my side, parents and brother and sister, from Sergei's side

Lina Prokofieva from Paris, his father Oleg S. Prokofiev with his eldest daughter from London. The wedding was celebrated in The Christian Community by the priest Hornemann whom Sergei had befriended. Karla Kiniger and her colleagues hosted the event, and Ursula Preuss was one of the witnesses. Unfortunately, it was not possible to invite Sergei's mother from Moscow. The following day all guests flew back to London, Sergei corrected the last pages with his translator, I conversed with Lina Prokofieva about her life; for the visa for Sergei could be extended only in the Russian Embassy in London on the basis of the marriage certificate valid in Britain. Somewhat timidly I went with Sergei to the strictly surveyed consulate. Dark expressions, checks of all papers, a verbal examination by the ambassador and a KGB officer followed, a long wait, dismissal pending further directives being received from Moscow. This meant days of uncertainty as to whether and when an extension of the visa would be possible.

Since the visitor's visa for England had ceased to be valid, Sergei decided not to wait around doing nothing and travelled with me to Tintagel on the west coast of England; and he called the embassy on a daily basis. The answer came only a week later in a timely fashion, that we should together make a second visit to the consulate to receive the marriage certificate that had now also been stamped by the Soviet Russian state and, hence, declared legally valid. He also received a visa for a further month's stay in Great Britain. Sergei remained in England with his family and newly acquired friends, whereas my next semester in Basel was beginning. We spent another weekend in Edinburgh and then I accompanied him with all his luggage on the train journey via Amsterdam for a brief stay in order to visit Rembrandt's house and to have a telephone conversation with Dan and Emma van Bemmelen, whom he knew from visits to Russia. In Eindhoven, the station on the border of Holland towards the East, Sergei got on to the through carriage to Moscow. He long recalled the rattling of the keys with which the guard of the carriage locked the doors of the train; now you are again locked in behind the Iron Curtain! The journey lasted two days and a night. Sergei had promised his mother and his anthroposophical friends to return, although all those belonging to Western families wanted to persuade him—all the more so now that he had a wife—to stay. He kept his word. He was uncertain whether his journey would be punished with harsh consequences.

His family received him warmly and the influential director of the Pushkin Museum in Moscow, his employer, welcomed him to his place as a valued art-historian and a guide of the galleries. Some time before, he had acquired a small one-room flat just for himself, which made my visits easier.

What began as a connection formed in heaven now had to mature through a deeper knowledge of one another and an inner probation in a three-year 'marriage at a distance'. Thus I was able to experience the Russian friends in their intense anthroposophical work, to acquire some rudimentary knowledge of Russian and on occasion—for example in a park—to meet his mother and the second wife of his maternal grandfather. Because of the place of work of Sergei's mother's husband and their daughter, I was prevented as a 'Western person' from visiting them at home.

When all my attempts to gain a possibility to stay in Moscow through work or marital connection came to grief through the dry indication 'only by acquiring Soviet Russian citizenship', Sergei sought permission to leave the country for Germany as the residence of his wife. In June 1985 he received this. It was very remarkable that, in spite of the strict political leadership under Andropov and subsequent General Secretaries, the regime did not initiate any persecution of the composer's grandson, his family and the anthroposophical friends, and the Western visitors and his wife were only surveyed. A good star of destiny was watching over him.

With a heavy heart Sergei's mother agreed to this decision, in the anxious conviction that she would not see her son again. She asked him to make regular telephone calls and to send a postcard from each place that he visited. Sergei with great joy sent her the most beautiful postcards with clearly written descriptions of his observations, numbered by journey in the hope that they would all get to her; for the Soviet censor and stamp collectors also had their interests. What rejoicing there was when with the year 1989 changes came about and Sergei made the journey to Moscow as soon as he could. Mutual visits between his and my families now became possible, but Sergei continued to write postcards to his mother from the most remote countries. Recently (2022) I spoke with her on the telephone, and she wanted to know the exact place in Brazil where we had been able to observe animals for a few days in the primeval forest in Parana and watch

Ursula Preuss (left) and Karla Kiniger were the two 'chosen grandmothers' of the young married couple. February 1982, Edinburgh

February 1982 in Edinburgh. On the left in the background from left to right: a friend of Anastasia's, Anastasia (half-sister to Sergei) and Lina Prokofieva

Family picture, 21 March 1982 in London shortly before his return to Russia. From left to right: Quentin †, Oleg Prokofiev, Lina Prokofieva, Anastasia, Gabriel, Astrid and Sergei Prokofieff

the crocodiles 'Callas' and 'Tchaikovsky'—as they were called, very skilfully eating the rest of our food from a hollow tree-trunk. How we spectators laughed at this circus! Only then did other animals emerge from the forest, in clear order of rank—foxes, rodents, vultures—to get their part of the food. It was lovely for me to hear the cheerful voice of Sergei's elderly mother who was full of the repeated memories of her son. She has kept all the postcards.

I filled the time of waiting for the exit permit with a further study of eurythmy in Dornach—a quiet wish of mine—which the Swiss authorities exceptionally granted. Thus from September 1985 Sergei was able to spend some years with me in Dornach building up his knowledge of the German language and continuing with the written work that he had begun, until with the conclusion of my studies in Dornach we both moved to Bad Boll-Eckwälden near Stuttgart in Germany, where his translator lived.

Now began his lecturing activity, in particular in 1988/89 with the theme of the cultural history of Russia to mark the 1,000-year jubilee of the Christianising of the Slavic people under Prince Vladimir in Kiev in the year 988. The books *The Spiritual Origins of Eastern Europe and the Future Mysteries of the Holy Grail* and *The Spiritual Tasks of Central and Eastern Europe* came to be written at this time, together with *The Heavenly Sophia and the Being Anthroposophia.*

* * *

Sergei was one of the first Russian anthroposophists who were able to make contact again with Western Europe after the Second World War. Thus a growing mutual understanding became possible through experiences and descriptions. The content of his lectures also helped him, as a bridge-builder between East and West, with his discernment. He regularly took part in the circle of those responsible for the anthroposophical work in the Stuttgart area, and he also participated in the branch work in Bad Boll-Eckwälden to the extent that his increasing travel permitted. The radical change in Russia from autumn 1989 led him to a new engagement of working with the now openly appearing anthroposophical groups throughout the country and fostering efforts towards the reopening of the Society in Russia. He made a decisive contribution in connection with the world Society and the Goetheanum in the formulating of the statutes. At Christmas 1990 there followed the legal entry of the Anthroposophical Society in Russia and the register of associations in Moscow. A conference for the festive opening, initiated by Sergei, took place in the hall of the House of the Composers in the middle of Moscow at St John's 1991 with numerous international guests. Many bonds were formed between the guests and Russian people, so that the anthroposophical daughter-movements, above all pedagogy, kindergarten, medicine, pharmaceutics and eurythmy and other arts could increasingly develop and firmly find their feet.

Our house in Bad Boll was the starting point of many lecture-tours, and their organization was my responsibility. Continuing studies and research for further publications took place with Dr Ursula Preuss as a remarkable translator and close friend. She was an adviser and a well-read anthroposophical conversation-partner. Sergei's own translating activity into Russian, for example of the texts of the Lessons of the Esoteric School, represented a further task. Our English-Austrian family friend Karla Kiniger urged him to improve his knowledge of English, since in future his journeys would take him to these regions of the world and it would be a hindrance to a fruitful connection with people if there had to be translations from Russian or German. It is a tribute to her skill that Sergei was able to give lectures in this language in Great Britain, Ireland and then also in the USA.

Special mention should be made of Sergei's meeting with one of the last people who knew Rudolf Steiner in their youth, Marjorie Spock. In the last 14 years of her life—and she was fully intellectually and spiritually active until the end of her 104 years—Sergei sought her out in Maine near Waterville whenever he visited the USA. A deep friendship arose between them.

When he was asked where he felt especially at home, Sergei answered:

> My physical home is in Moscow, where I was born. Through the connection of my grandfather Leonid Feinberg with Maximilian Voloshin—both were painters—the way was prepared for me to be able to encounter anthroposophy there. My soul home is in Koktebel, in Voloshin's house, where I was able to experience his second wife Maria Stepanovna Voloshina. As a seven-year-old child and especially from my fourteenth year I visited her once or twice every year, for longer in the summer and also in the New Year holidays. She

> became for me like a second grandmother. An intensive correspondence nurtured the connection between us. My spiritual home is Dornach, the work-place of Rudolf Steiner.

After his death in 1932, Maximilian Voloshin's house in Koktebel continued to be a place where artists and the intelligentsia—above all from St Petersburg and Moscow—met, where they shared their poems and paintings and spent stimulating holidays together in conversation with one another. Sergei was able to immerse himself in this circle and met people there both old and young in age and also those with philosophical interests. There is still some contact today with a few who like him chose the path to anthroposophy, for example Elena Domratshova, whom destiny led to a Waldorf School in Stuttgart as a eurythmy teacher. The fateful meeting in this house with Vladislav Ivonin in the summer of 1973 enabled him to make contacts with further friends in St Petersburg. Thus it was from the anthroposophical writings in Voloshin's house that he came to know of Rudolf Steiner's lectures, of which translations were available. Only later did the connection with the anthroposophical friends in Moscow arise. In St Petersburg there were still some elderly people who had met Rudolf Steiner when they were young. Sergei visited them quietly. Also later on his journeys he took a real interest in looking for such people, speaking with them and seeing the inner fire from the meeting with Rudolf Steiner shine forth. Sergei had also kindled this fire within himself. In the 1990s, he was accordingly asked to give courses about Rudolf Steiner and the development of anthroposophy at the Priests' Seminar in Stuttgart.

In meeting with Russian anthroposophists, I have been particularly struck by the existential relationship that each of them has with anthroposophy. Every weekly meeting was an inner source of life for them which radiated through the week until the next such evening. This applied especially to Sergei, who orientated his whole life around it and took great risks. His profession was to be 'an anthroposophist'. It was therefore a piece of good fortune that he was granted permission to leave Soviet Russia and could become active in 'Western' Europe through further publications and beginning his lecture-tours. A day without intensive study and working with anthroposophcal content made him sad; he clearly lacked something that nourished him.

The years in Bad Boll were happy and full of creative cheer. We could both finance our material needs with our different tasks and Sergei, as an independent author and lecturer, was increasingly invited by anthroposophical branches and country Societies worldwide. His themes were manifold. But his central concern was the Foundation Stone Meditation, the Christmas Conference of 1923 and Rudolf Steiner's life in all its various aspects. Many personal friendships were established, as, for example, to the Paracelsus branch in Basel and to René Harrer, who invited him for annual lecturing weekends over a period of ten years.

It was my task to organize the journeys, to deal with the correspondence by dictation, some manuscripts were dictated to me, the house and garden needed caring for with Sergei's occasional assistance, alongside eurythmy lessons in the kindergarten, courses for amateurs and eurythmy performances for children in the therapeutic educational institute of Eckwälden together with local colleagues. It was for me an inwardly very fulfilling and enriching activity. It was especially good when I was able to come with him on one or another journey and get to know distant lands and their people; Israel and Egypt, several times Moscow and St Petersburg with regular courses from me in kindergarten training in both places and lectures by Sergei in his mother tongue. What a different person was standing there then, as though veiled in a different soul-spiritual mantle, someone who was able in a free, creative way to imbue his thoughts with poetic and humour-filled words while carefully shaping the moods of his listeners. A great journey to Mumbai and Australia comprising various places, then an extensive journey through New Zealand, Manila in the Philippines and several places where anthroposophical work is going on in Japan—I could accompany him and occasionally contribute something of a musical or eurythmical nature to the seminars and lectures. Everything was carefully planned by the representatives of the country Societies. Many sights of the cultures and the natural environment were opened up to us. I was also able to accompany him on a lecture-tour through South America—Brazil, Argentina, Peru—and on two occasions through various places in the USA and also Toronto. We visited the great waterfalls of the Earth. Sergei could form an intensive connection with nature and loved to move silently within it, perceiving life in all its many forms. On a walk near the

Grand Canyon in the Red Rocks for example, he encountered a rattlesnake a few yards away from him which he observed without fear, then with presence of mind he jumped from stone to stone away from it to us on the path. Our stamping and shouting drove it away. Journeys in Scandinavia with conferences in Järna on, for example, the theme of the eurythmy forms for the Foundation Stone Meditation with the Swedish stage group, also enabled us to get to know these countries and their people more closely. A wonderful voyage by ship from Bergen to Hammerfest with a stay at Lofoten was associated with lectures in Oslo, Tromsö, Bergen and Lillehammer.

The following memory also belongs to the 1990s. When Sergei's youngest half-sister and brother, Beatrice and Rupert, could still barely run (Sergei's father Oleg had made a journey to England in 1972, had remained there and had six children with his third wife Frances), we were invited to Oleg and Frances's house in London for a shared Christmas festival. Sergei took delight in the very tasty English Christmas pies and especially the Christmas pudding, which has to be served flambé and hot (with brandy butter for grown-ups). The day was filled with the most diverse preparations. Oleg had made some last purchases and Sergei skilfully set up the tree, the older sister and brother, Anastasia and Gabriel, decorated it—with Sergei as big brother, who did duty for the ladder—with chains of lights, glass balls, coloured birds and other decorations with much hilarity for a festive splendour. Gabriel tried out his trumpet prelude. Cordelia as a five-year-old girl jumped to and fro amongst everyone, waiting impatiently for Christmas Eve to begin. Frances calmly surveyed the scene and looked after the twins. Finally a friend brought a big lasagne, which only had to be warmed up while we all gathered around the tree, sang songs, listened to Gabriel's trumpet solo—rendered with conviction—and exchanged gifts. This was concluded, in the English fashion, with Christmas crackers and merry surprises. Then came the dinner, when all gathered around a big table, the younger children surrounded their big brother, who fully engaged them in conversation in English. Frances, Oleg and I looked after the little ones. Sergei excitedly awaited the pudding being cooked in the oven. He wanted to see how the pudding was 'set alight'. The high-proof brandy was an effective help. Everyone took pleasure in the tongues of flame, which all too quickly went out. Sergei, who loved fire, then with Gabriel prepared a real fire in the living room, where he described to the children how a Russian Christmas is celebrated.

The relationship between the various brothers and sisters has grown since then, also through the unexpectedly early death of Oleg in the summer of 1998, when Sergei could very helpfully stand by Frances's side. Gabriel developed into a world-famous musician and his visits to Moscow always included meetings with Sophia Leonidovna, her daughter Maria, Sergei's half-sister, and her family, husband Yuri and daughter Nastya. Over the years, a real bond has grown between the families, thanks mainly to Sergei and Gabriel.

Remarkably, the death of Sergei's stepfather, Victor, also occurred in the autumn of the same year. In November 1998, Sergei and I travelled to Moscow for a farewell visit, since a stroke had greatly weakened him. His loving smile and the intimate glance of this otherwise reserved scientist touched me deeply. He made Russian more accessible to me with the beautiful rhyming fairy tale 'Konyok Garbunok' by Pyotr Ershov. During long winter evenings, he had himself built a telescope with a hand-polished mirror and with all its various parts for Sergei as a teenager in his work-place as a physicist. He accompanied Sergei to Switzerland. I said goodbye to Victor with a gratefully intimate handshake, which Sophia noticed with sympathetic interest. Then, as the son of a loving stepfather, Sergei said farewell to him on his own.

* * *

In my close collaboration with Sergei, not even his considerable reserve could conceal from me that by the end of the 1990s an increasing tension was developing within him. He was speaking all over the world about the most essential tasks of anthroposophy and of the Anthroposophical Society. And yet he was like a 'guest' in the anthroposophical movement and was only occasionally invited to give a lecture at the Goetheanum, as, for example, in July 2000 for the conference 'The World Religions from the Standpoint of Anthroposophy'. It was as if Sergei, speaking from the heart of the Anthroposophical Society, was able to awaken inner impulses in the souls of those listening for which, it seemed, they had long been waiting. On his travels he was sometimes asked: 'Why are you not involved at the Goetheanum?'

When he was asked to join the Vorstand (Executive Council) of the General Anthroposophical Society at the Goetheanum in 2001, our life changed. He acquired a professional secretary, the well-practised work-forms of the Vorstand were embraced. Sergei joyfully greeted every colleague whom he encountered with a handshake, and included the guests and visitors, also the little children. Unfortunately, his entry to the Vorstand was overshadowed by a longstanding crisis of a legal nature in the Society. Nevertheless, it appeared to many friends from outside that a new, warm impulse was emanating from this place through his presence in the Vorstand and his contributions at conferences. He constantly endeavoured to keep abreast with an extensive correspondence, sometimes posing detailed anthroposophical questions. With time, however, a deeper gulf of irreconcilable views and intentions between individual members of the Vorstand manifested itself, which for Sergei constituted an increasing difficulty. Always making every effort to work together collegially, he found it difficult to bear. And yet the inner commitment to be responsible to the exoteric and esoteric Anthroposophical Society created by Rudolf Steiner was to him so binding that he could not resign from his office without existential reasons, which only emerged as a result of his serious illness from 2011 onwards.

In spite of his illness, his daily efforts were dedicated to the books that he had promised to anthroposophists. His beautiful house in Dornach offered him the necessary peace. His secretary Ute Fischer stood helpfully by his side. Fortunately, the medical attention and other care could—apart from some stays in hospital—take place as an out-patient or at home, which was a great saving for his forces and for his feeling for life. These were further special years in which I could accompany him on his path. A deep gratitude connects me with Sergei in heartfelt love for his being that has so early been taken from us.

Heinrich Schneider

An Art Expedition to Moscow

Towards the middle of the 1980s, my wife and I were visiting some historical places in the then Soviet Union as participants of a German-speaking group led by an experienced travel-guide from

Switzerland. It had also been planned to see an old church in an outlying quarter of Moscow, but on this occasion accompanied not by a Soviet tourist guide from Intourist but by a Russian who was personally known to our Swiss travel-guide and whom he had privately asked to do this. We were therefore excited to meet this art specialist whose name had not been mentioned.

So now we—approximately 30 people from Switzerland and Germany—were standing in this Moscow church with its old frescoes. Suddenly the promised 'art expert' came into our midst: a tall young man, with dark clothes and a black, broad-brimmed hat. He led us in good German into the spiritual background of the old, ecclesiastical art and proved to be highly competent and motivated. We listened to what he said with a growing sense of admiration. Some of the participants would dearly have liked to have asked more questions. But the young man had disappeared as abruptly as he had appeared while we were recalling what he had just said for a brief moment in a mood of grateful silence. Then we heard an elderly member of our party asking near us with a quiet voice: 'Who is this? Is he a priest?' It was Sergei O. Prokofieff.

Sergei and Astrid in the middle of the 1980s in Moscow. Photograph by Heinrich Schneider

Sergei O. Prokofieff's book *Rudolf Steiner and the Founding of the New Mysteries* had appeared in German in Stuttgart three years before, an uncensored and therefore illegal publication in the West, which was at that time strictly forbidden by the Soviet government. In order not to further endanger the author of the book, his name was concealed. He himself, undeterred by all dangers, was nevertheless then following the anthroposophical path that he had discerned in accordance with the aims of Gods.

Paul and Ulrike Mackay

Early Connections and Later Collaboration

I came to know Sergei in the spring of 1982 in the parental home of his wife Astrid in Bonn. I was then living in Bochum and was invited to an opportunity to meet Sergei after he had been in Dornach at Christmas 1981. My future wife, Ulrike, had already got to know Sergei in Moscow, where in 1981/82 she studied for a few months at the Pushkin Institute. I already knew Astrid from the time when Jörgen Smit was responsible for the Youth Section.

Ulrike and I then journeyed to Moscow in August 1982 together with a travel group that included Astrid and Karla Kiniger. It was for me a wonderful opportunity to meet Sergei in his home country. I learned to appreciate his warm-heartedness, his love of life but also his wakefulness with regard to telephone tapping and surveillance. We practised some Schubert songs for an evening when the anthroposophical friends met together in his home. Astrid and I sang, Ulrike accompanied. Then Sergei came into the room where we were practising, and said: 'This evening you really must sing!' We asked: 'Why?' He answered with a mischievous smile: 'Because it will be well received!' He was a person who had learnt to make the most out of difficult circumstances.

From 1983 until 1987 we were living in the Netherlands. From this time I can remember a visit that Sergei made to our house. He had given a lecture in Zurich and came to us afterwards. We had a fireplace in our living room, and Sergei loved to be beside an open fire. We entered into a scintillating conversation concerned not only with matters of spiritual significance but also with human concerns. He could, for example, relate well to our children. He once went for a walk in the forest with Ulrike and our children. He carried the younger one for a while on his shoulders. The older one was keen to do the same, but he had in the meantime wet his pants. Sergei accordingly looked at him as if to say that this would unfortunately not be possible.

In the summer of 1991 Jörgen Smit wanted to hold the nineteen Lessons of the School of Spiritual Science in Järna to mark the opening of the great hall in the new anthroposophical building. Unfortunately, he became ill in January 1991 and therefore asked four people to take on the Lessons for him. In addition to Arne Klingborg, Jörgen Smit asked Michaela Glöckler, Sergei and me. He died on 10 May 1991. The four of us then had to make the best of holding the Lessons. Michaela, Sergei and I were relatively new to this work. It was a wonderful opportunity to get to know one another through this work. In this way a deep spiritual relationship arose that was for me also important as a foundation for our later work together.

From 2001 until 2012 Sergei and I were able to work together in the Executive Council of the Anthroposophical Society. Our fields of activity were very different. For Sergei it was a relatively new experience to work together with colleagues in a committee. In the early autumn of 2010 he spoke about this and was grateful to have been allowed to experience this form of collegiality.

In 2011 Sergei became ill and therefore decided to withdraw from his work on the Vorstand. On 26 July 2014 Sergei died. On 27 July Virginia Sease and I were able to visit him in the library of his house, where he was laid out.

Nicholas Nunhofer

Gifts of an East-European to People from the West

I first became acquainted with Sergei Prokofieff's work in 1988 at the age of 19, when I found his first book in the old English Section headquarters near the British Museum which is also where Rudolf Steiner Press was located at that time. I should like to recall the atmosphere of that time that I felt around him.

This was one of great excitement; great interest and great expectation as well. (Linked into this was the fact that back then there was, from certain points of view, still 'all to play for' as far as Rudolf Steiner's 'Michael prophecy' concerning the end of the twentieth century was concerned.) I had many profound encounter-type experiences with this first book of his and absolutely loved the copy I had. For me this book was a godsend at that time.

This prepared me to see him in September 1990 when he came to Britain to deliver a great lecture on the coming of the Etheric Christ and the Foundation Stone Meditation. During the course of this lecture I intuitively sensed that the complicated and profound imagination which he described in this lecture (to do with spiritual beings associated with the Foundation Stone Meditation) was something that he had personally experienced. I experienced him as a Grail bearer, bearing the Grail of the new mysteries (the Foundation Stone Meditation) from the East to the West. I also experienced the deep affinity between his connection to the Foundation Stone and his connection to Rudolf Steiner. I felt during this time—and this thought has only increased (been further substantiated) over the years—that his own connection to the Foundation Stone Meditation had something of the nature of co-creator/initiator of this with Rudolf Steiner from the spiritual world.

While speaking of his Grail mission, I should also like to mention the 'Russia' book here that contains this word in its title and relates so much to this theme (and was published around this time, 1989).

A few weeks later, in November 1990, I was in Germany and attended a conference in Witten where he spoke (Jörgen Smit was also there). During a working group he was asked by a participant to talk about the relationship one had with anthroposophy behind the Iron Curtain. He said that this is something special that should not be lost, although he added that his own experience was extremely modest. Nevertheless, I felt very strongly that his relationship to anthroposophy had something to do with these conditions (as he describes in the Preface to his book on the being Anthroposophia) and that this is an important part of his legacy to us who live in the West and have known external freedoms all our lives but nonetheless live in a spiritual atmosphere ever more akin to that of Russia under Bolshevism.

Being still somewhat connected externally with anthroposophy during this time (up to the mid-1990s) I became aware of his isolation and also of the lack of active engagement with his work in any serious way—especially amongst some of the leading figures—but also in general. I found this distressing and could not really understand it in any other than very negative terms. When I read in his summary from January 2014 that his intentions on joining the Vorstand were not realized 'even in a preliminary way' I was profoundly affected and shocked (but not surprised). Clearly his isolation had remained and maybe even intensified with the departure of the older generations.

For me he strove not merely to maintain the existence of anthroposophy on the Earth but also to try to realize the spirit of the new esoteric impulse born after the Christmas Conference—to continue in this sense where Steiner had perforce to leave it. He lived his whole life out of this impulse, and I feel that this is his legacy. Perhaps this is the cross on which he died. This is how I would like to remember him.

1984, still in the underground. Back row, from left to right: Vanya Demel, Vitali Kovalenko, Elena Luchkina, Ira Surkova, Pyotr Chaikovsky. Middle row: Zhenya, Bondarev's first wife, Ala Ragozhina, Sergei Prokofieff, Astrid Prokofieff, Natasha Kovalenko, Vladimir Tikhomirov. In the forground: Tatyana Pirogova, Boris Nozov

Sevak Edward Gulbekian

Reminiscences of Sergei O. Prokofieff

It began and ended with some difficult correspondence—although initially it wasn't directed to me.

I was a new graduate who had landed a precious first job in publishing at Rudolf Steiner Press, then based in grand offices in Bloomsbury, a stone's throw from the British Museum. It was a week before my 23rd birthday. Although I had spent some years in a Waldorf School, I knew nothing of anthroposophy—but I was to learn fast. During my first week, the manager passed me a series of freshly-translated lectures by Rudolf Steiner and told me to edit them.

At the time of my arrival, the in-house editor was proofing a debut title by a young Russian who had only recently emerged from the Soviet Union. The German edition of the book had already stirred up strong feelings in readers, and—as I was to learn—there was growing anticipation around the forthcoming English edition. It was, of course, Sergei Prokofieff's *Rudolf Steiner and the Founding of the New Mysteries*[12] —arguably, the most profoundly esoteric book to be published since Rudolf Steiner's death.

Following publication, a letter from the author arrived at the office. It complained, justifiably, about the shoddy production quality of the new book. Among other faults, it was poorly bound and the numbers jumped randomly from the outer to the inner corners of the page. The letter aroused some consternation among the senior staff. A reply had to be composed and it needed to look professional. This called for the office computer, a monolithic machine that no one really knew how to use. As a youngster with some experience of the novel technology, I was called upon to take dictation, and thus I came to type my first letter to Sergei Prokofieff.

* * *

My initial glimpse of Sergei followed a couple of years later. I had resigned from the chaotically-managed Press and escaped to Australia

[12]The first edition incorrectly gives the date of publication as 1986. It was in fact 1987.

for a working holiday. Following that antipodean stint, I found myself in Dornach, working as a temporary stagehand at the Goetheanum. It was summer, and Sergei was scheduled to give a lecture in the great hall on the subject of forgiveness.[13] Every seat in the house was taken and there was a buzz of excitement around the place. Armed with only my school-boy German and what I had managed to pick up whilst in Switzerland, I nevertheless felt that I understood the essence of what Sergei was saying. In particular, I was deeply impressed by his earnestness and passion, which were amply evident. With youthful exhilaration, I felt strongly that he was speaking truth! This was someone I could believe in. Little did I know that in less than a year I would be his publisher.

* * *

I was called back to England with the offer of an assistant's job at a fledgling publishing enterprise at the Temple Lodge Christian Community in Hammersmith, West London. Sergei's close friend, Karla Kiniger, had discovered Temple Lodge as a replacement publisher and they had already brought out his second book, *The Twelve Holy Nights and the Spiritual Hierarchies*. But months after I arrived, the manager departed and the trustees resolved to close the publishing department. I was kept on for administrative purposes, but managed to talk the trustees into giving me a chance to keep the publishing going, with the understanding that there would be no more financial support. The translated manuscript of Sergei's third book, *The Cycle of the Year as a Path of Initiation*, had arrived in the interim. A vast work, my first task was to find a way to get it copy-edited...

A couple of months later, Sergei arrived in London with his wife Astrid to give some lectures around the United Kingdom. They stayed in the guesthouse at Temple Lodge and I was to meet them the following morning. I hardly slept that night. I wasn't sure what to expect but was full of nervous anticipation. The meeting took place on a sunny spring morning and was warm and relaxed. As a Russian, he was intrigued by my Armenian heritage, and over lunch we talked animatedly on many subjects.

[13]The content was later expanded into his well-known work, *The Occult Significance of Forgiveness*.

The world was a very different place. The Berlin Wall had just fallen and the Soviet Union was close to collapse. There was optimism in the air. We were both at the beginning of our literary careers—Sergei in his mid-thirties and I in my mid-twenties.

* * *

A couple of years later, Sergei was back in London to give an evening presentation at Rudolf Steiner House in Baker Street. I was to accompany him, and I thought it would display an egalitarian spirit to travel there via the underground system. As we walked through the crowded train searching for a seat, Sergei—resplendent in a three-piece suit—almost tripped over a passenger's outstretched leg. I felt ashamed.

The following day, I planned to take Sergei to the weird and wonderful Festival of Mind, Body & Spirit in central London, then a yearly event. This time I phoned for a cab. The firm's publicity card promised luxury vehicles. In the event, a beaten-up old car turned up. I felt I was being taught a lesson.

At the Festival, there was a stall promoting a new movement based around a rather odd-looking individual who believed he was an incarnation of the highest divine entity. As we left the hall, Sergei giggled like a child at the notion that *that* man supposed he was God…!

* * *

Some years later, I drove Sergei to Devon where he was to give a talk. He wanted to visit the hall in Torquay where Rudolf Steiner had given his famous lectures on 'True and False Paths in Initiation', among others. Someone from the local anthroposophical group had kindly arranged with the town's council for us to have access to the hall at a specific time. The young woman who showed us round seemed somewhat bemused and was curious to know why we wanted to see the building. She mentioned that the previous weekend it had been rented out for the local 'flea market'. Sergei explained, calmly, that we were members of a spiritual group whose leader had given some important lectures at this very place. I was impressed by his matter-of-fact explanation. Later, facing the sea, we ate fish and chips. Sergei liberally applied his with tomato ketchup.

* * *

Another time, Sergei invited me to Järna in Sweden, where he was to give a series of lectures in English at a conference. I was able to take my partner and young family. One evening, under the strong light of the long Scandinavian evenings, Sergei took us for a walk, describing how the land we trod had previously been underwater for many centuries. He hoisted my toddler-daughter onto his shoulders, where she stayed, happily, for the duration of the excursion.

* * *

On a family holiday in Germany and Switzerland, I arranged to visit Sergei, who was then on the Executive Council of the Society. He took us on a personal tour around Dornach, obtaining keys to see the sculpted 'Group' statue as well as the room in which Rudolf Steiner had died. He took us to his house where, over apple juice and chocolate, he described with enthusiasm his recent visit to Easter Island (Rapa Nui). Later, he took us to a pizza restaurant where, utilizing the knives at the table, he initiated a 'sword fight' with my youngest daughters.

* * *

More than once I heard Sergei sincerely ask the question: 'Where are my contemporaries?' I don't think I truly understood the extraordinary nature of this utterance at the time—although it is reflected in the 'loneliness' that others have spoken of. My sense is that Sergei found one of these 'contemporaries' quite late on in his career in the form of Peter Selg, with whom he gratefully collaborated. Clearly, they had a deep appreciation of each other's work, and became colleagues and friends.

* * *

In April 2013, our final encounter in the flesh, Sergei was already very ill. I was in Dornach on business. Battles were taking place within the Anthroposophical Society in Great Britain, with nakedly political intentions. My own position was under threat and, curiously, I had difficulty making an appointment to visit Sergei. Impertinently, I knocked on the front door of his home. Sergei was surprised but pleased to see me, graciously welcoming me with a warm hug. We talked for a couple of hours and he described at some length his attendance—together with his extended family—at recent celebrations for his grandfather Sergei Prokofiev, the famous composer. He also told me about the book he had just written entitled *Time Journeys*. I asked him why—given the international recognition and world-historic positioning of his grandfather—his own destiny had led him to write a book that challenged the work of a fellow anthroposophist, within this small community. How had it come to this? Without rancour, he told me that someday he would tell me. Sadly, that day never came.

* * *

Back in England, I had received a credible legal threat over the publication of *Time Journeys*. Although I didn't share this with him, the Chair of Temple Lodge Publishing's trustees, a lawyer by profession, had independently concluded that we could not publish the book. This was due to Britain's weak libel laws, putting the burden of proof on the defendant. We had already published Sergei's critiques of Alice Bailey, Nicholas and Helena Roerich and—most controversially—Valentin Tomberg. The difference with all these books, however, was that the individuals concerned were dead. Nevertheless, as one might expect, the decision to decline publication of this latest work led to some animosity, and possibly even feelings of betrayal.

The above events resulted in the difficult correspondence mentioned at the outset of this article. And so, after a period of 24 years during which time we had published over 30 of Sergei's books in English translation—our role was replaced. It was an ignominious end to the relationship.

* * *

Following Sergei's passing in 2014, an understanding was reached with Astrid Prokofieff, which led to the publication by Temple Lodge of several posthumous books, including the one you have in your hands.

1985–2014: DORNACH, GERMANY, JOURNEYS

Virginia Sease

Sergei O. Prokofieff's Work in the Executive Council at the Goetheanum

Sergei, Whitsun 1992 in Koktebel. Photo: E. Glazachova

At the time when Sergeij Prokofieff was called to join the Executive Council in the year 2001, the members of the Executive Council were Manfred Schmidt-Brabant, President (as of 1975), Virginia Sease, Secretary (as of 1984), Heinz Zimmermann, Recording Secretary (as of 1988), Rolf Kerler, Treasurer (as of 1988) and Paul Mackay (as of 1996). Considerations concerning further appointments to the Executive Council accompany the work of the Council, sometimes quietly and at other times quite actively. The principle of augmentation for the Executive Council does not depend upon succession, but from the aspect of continuity in the work of the Anthroposophical Society, the School for Spiritual Science and for the Goetheanum. Each one of us in the Executive Council already had had meetings and perceptions of Sergei Prokofieff, as we were aware of his presence through his lectures and books, at that time especially in Europe. An initial acquaintance with a future colleague already prepares a basis for the possibility of a later closer cooperation in anthroposophy and in the General Anthroposophical Society.

My own first perception of Sergei Prokofieff came in 1982 through an early morning telephone call to me in Los Angeles from Germany—in Europe it was already evening. A friend from Stuttgart phoned and with great enthusiasm told me about an event in Stuttgart. Through the 'grapevine' she had heard that a young Russian would give a lecture about the Foundation Stone verse and the task of anthroposophy. The name of the lecturer was not allowed to be mentioned publicly. The hall of the large Stuttgart Waldorf Schule at Uhlandshöhe was filled to the last seat. Ursula Preuss, Ph.D. greeted the lecturer in the name of the Anthroposophical Society in Stuttgart. The young Russian spoke in German without any notes. At the request of the audience at the conclusion he recited the Foundation Stone verse in Russian. Else Klink's Eurythmy Ensemble performed the Foundation Stone verse. It might be that I was the first person in America who immediately heard about this event—6,000 miles away. It was, however, not the first appearance of Sergei Prokofieff in west Europe. On the way back from England to Russia, he was able to make a detour into Switzerland and Germany. He had received a special waiver permission to visit his father in England, but the trip should have been directly from Moscow to London and back to Moscow. Of course, such an undertaking at that time was extremely dangerous. He arrived in Dornach on 23 December, 1981 and Annie Jahn, who knew him from Moscow, received him as a guest. Astrid Seufert, his future wife, met him at this time. Her father already was acquainted with him, because as of the 1970s he visited Moscow regularly in order to work there with the anthroposophical friends. When Sergei arrived in Dornach it was so foggy that he could only touch the Goetheanum and not see it at all! He attended the Christmas Conference with the performances of the four Mystery Dramas by Rudolf Steiner and also with lectures by members of the Executive Council. After the performances Jörgen Smit, who was a member of the Executive Council and also the leader of the Youth Section, could arrange for Sergei Prokofieff to give some lectures about the rhythms of the Foundation Stone verse in connection with life after death. This event took place in the student dormitory. Prior to this a conversation with the Executive Council—Friedrich Hiebel, Rudolf Grosse, Jörgen Smit, Manfred Schmidt Brabant, Hagen Biesantz and Gisela Reuther—had occurred. The attendance at the lectures was very good. At that time Johannes Händler and his wife, Veronika, were responsible for the student dormitory and every evening after the Conference in the Goetheanum, they arranged everything which was necessary for Sergei Prokofieff's lectures. The late hour was not a disturbance for the enthusiastic attendees.

In the 1990s the question was often considered as to whether Sergei Prokofieff would be called to join the Executive Council. There were considerations concerning how he could work from the Goetheanum. It was self-understood that he would bring good impulses, but it would lead to a great change in his life. When one assumes internal and external responsibility for the Goethanum as a building, as headquarters of the General Anthroposophical Society and the School for Spiritual Science, these tasks require a renunciation of a major part of one's 'free time', which was available before for one's own research.

In the last meeting before the summer recess in the year 2000 the unanimous decision of the Council resulted in the request to Sergei Prokofieff to become a member of the Executive Council. I presented our request to him in August with the wish that he could consider it and respond by Michaelmas. At the same time, also Bodo von Plato and Cornelius Pietzner were invited to weigh this possibility. Sergei Prokofieff received the request calmly and responded that he would reflect upon it and would inform us on time. In reflecting after 21 years [this original German contribution was in 2022] especially one aspect of this call stands time-wise in an important context. The decision occurred at the time when Manfred Schmidt-Brabant was not yet ill. The fact that he died seven months later formed the constellation of the Executive Council differently than we originally had considered. For the first time and in a natural, consequential manner the geographic regions of the northern hemisphere would have been represented in the Executive Council: Virginia Sease from the west of the United States, Sergei Prokofieff from eastern Europe, Paul Mackay from Holland, Cornelius

Pietzner from the east of the United States, Heinz Zimmermann from Switzerland, Manfred Schmidt-Brabant and Bodo von Plato from Germany (Cornelius Pietzner could only take up this task as of 2002). Through the unexpected departure of Manfred Schmidt-Brabant, this balance, especially through the central representation of Germany by means of two personalities, could not be realized.

The initiatives and impulses which Sergei Prokofieff brought into the work at the Goetheanum and throughout the world arising from the Anthroposophical Society and the School for Spiritual Science are manifold and can only be mentioned in a limited and sketchy manner. Also, his many publications and books cannot be enumerated as they would well exceed the limitations of this contribution. Significant anthroposophical presses, such as Verlag Freies Geistesleben in Stuttgart, published his works. But in the Executive Council we were especially pleased that as of 1986 the Verlag (publisher) am Goetheanum could publish most of his works.

Right after Sergei Prokofieff had commenced with his task at the Goetheanum, he joined the other members of the Executive Council and the leaders of the various Sections in an initiative for members of the Society and members of the First Class of the School for Spiritual Science. It was characterized as 'Winter Work on Monday'. After several years the weekly rhythm between October to April was no longer possible from time considerations for some members of the Council and Section Leaders, until finally only two groups met regularly—those of Sergei Prokofieff and Virginia Sease. The latter group works still today with Oliver Conradt and Claus-Peter Röh. But also several new constellations of Executive Council members and Section Leaders were inspired by this impulse and for some time worked further. Since this work was conversational following an introduction, many members experienced another aspect of Sergei Prokofieff. They knew him from his lectures and books, now they could experience him as another human being, who could formulate questions and insights of the participants into the nature of a conversation, as well as this was possible with 70 participants!

After Sergei Prokofieff commenced his work in the Executive Council, he introduced an impulse which continued then for a number of years: at the yearly Christmas Conference on Christmas Day, he read Rudolf Steiner's words for the Laying of the Foundation Stone of the

Anthroposophical Society from 25 December, 1923. Before the reading he gave an introduction.

He continued with this impulse until 2011 and the Anthroposophical Society in Switzerland carried it further. For many years he was responsible for the commemoration events connected with the birthday and the death day of Rudolf Steiner. He brought often less known facts concerning Rudolf Steiner's inner and outer work.

Every year Friedrich Hiebel, a member of the Executive Council and the leader of the Humanities Section (*Sektion für Schöne Wissenschaften*), until his death in 1989, created a conference for the Whitsun Festival. The Whitsun Conference continued to take place under changing directors, as part of the Humanities Section. Today it is carried by Christiane Haid, Leader of the Humanities Section. For the time of Ascension, however, the situation was different: there was neither a conference nor a festival for Ascension. Sergei Prokofieff recognized the need to also consider this time. The conferences which he initiated for the time of Ascension encompassed vital aspects of anthroposophy, for example *The Philosophy of Freedom*, *Esoteric Science, an Outline*, the *Fifth Gospel* and the *Christmas Conference 1923/24*. His last great conference at Ascension took place from 6–8 May, 2011, with the comprehensive theme 'The Alchemy of the Forces of the Soul' connected with Rudolf Steiner's three meditations: 'The Butterfly Meditation' (Falter Meditation), the 'Warmth-Meditation' and the 'Michael-Imagination'. In addition to Sergei Prokofieff also Florian Roder and Peter Selg were active.

On the occasion of the Annual General Meeting of the General Anthroposophical Society in April 2011 Sergei O. Prokofieff was affirmed by the members for the second time as a member of the Executive Council with a huge majority.

Sergei O. Prokofieff as a Colleague

He was always a good colleague—but to say this as regarding a colleague is not sufficient. How was he a good colleague, what stands behind that, what does that include? Each Executive Council member from that time would approach this question individually. The following can only describe briefly how I experienced him as a colleague who especially valued cooperation.

For conferences at the Goetheanum in which contributions for the same theme were divided up among us, Sergei Prokofieff was always willing to offer lectures and conversation groups. This marked a significant aspect for the quality of the conference, because it led thematically to a united endeavour. Also, one felt free in one's own preparation regarding the choice of an important theme, which could be contributed from individual research. In case one needed a reference, Sergei was always helpful, as he had a comprehensive knowledge of Rudolf Steiner's lectures and publications. This knowledge extended also to related works, not only in German, but also in English, French and of course, Russian. He also was familiar with many great works in world literature.

Sergei Prokofieff was often silent during meetings, until it became clear for him how he could bring clarity to a theme on the agenda through a supplementary contribution. Sometimes it concerned a correction involving a criticism, which he could prove with facts, or with an indication of a publication which he considered as not compatible with anthroposophy. He also brought humour into our meetings.

After over 1,000 members had affirmed the continuation of his work in the Executive Council in 2011, an illness occurred in a dramatic manner. His work in the Executive Council had to be interrupted. In the autumn of 2011, he held his last lectures about the biography of Rudolf Steiner in commemoration of his 150th birth year.

He entered into a path of suffering with many treatments. On 10 November, 2012, it was nevertheless possible for him to participate in a meeting of the Executive Council and we experienced ourselves once again as a wholeness; also on 14 and 15 January, 2013 he could be present for parts of the meeting, at which time he informed us that he would have to relinquish his work. His health was such that no recovery was possible; it was only the question of a limited extension of his life, which left us in deep sadness. After a handshake with each one of us we left the meeting room in silence. On 19 February, 2013, he briefly attended a meeting with the Section Leaders with the members of the Executive Council and also took leave of this group.

In retrospect, special qualities of Sergei Prokofieff stand before me. In the work in the Executive Council, as well as with the Collegium of the School for Spiritual Science, when essential questions in relation to the Goetheanum as a building were considered, his love for the maintenance and care of this building resounded with great energy; according to the intentions of Rudolf Steiner our task and responsibility lay in remaining as faithful to the building as possible. His stance in this matter sometimes led to contrary feelings among the colleagues; he allowed this to come towards him without justifying his conviction, but also without giving in, just to achieve a superficial harmony. From my observation, inner and outer honesty as a main quality of his character were always completely present. He never bore a grudge. He understood his task as a member of the Executive Council to work further for the impulses of the Anthroposophical Society and the School for Spiritual Science as Rudolf Steiner, as an initiate, wished them to be realized. As these initiatives never could or should depend on one person, he strove to work for them mutually with his colleagues. His point of departure centred on the fact that the Anthroposophical Society first of all must be perceived as an esoteric Society and from there, as it may be possible, to carry deeds into the public domain. His numerous publications which today are also available in many translations, bear witness to this interpretation of his work. Although he completely understood the situation it was painful for him that his colleagues rarely occupied themselves with his works or read them due to time constraints. They were written by him out of the centre of anthroposophy—he did not write them for himself, or as a hobby, but for the world in which the Goetheanum exists and works. In contrast, he was very aware of the work and the activities of his colleagues, which often came as a surprise when he referred to them.

At the end of his life Sergei Prokofieff wrote two comprehensive works about the School for Spiritual Science. Two members of the Executive Council mentioned this in a letter to him in June 2014.

> Dear Sergei,
>
> … We greatly regret that due to your health situation it is not possible to engage in the planned conversation with you about your second book concerning the School for Spiritual Science.[14] We deeply respect the fact that despite your illness you could finish this book and we look forward to the time when we can enter into it. (…) Unfortunately, instead of a direct conversation with you, nevertheless we hope that

---

[14]Sergei O. Prokofieff, *The Esoteric Path through the Nineteen Class Lessons in the Light of the Supersensible Mystery of Golgotha and the Fifth Gospel*, Stuttgart, 2016. Available through the Hochschulsekretariat at the Goetheanum, hochschule@goetheanum.ch.

> in receiving the content of your book an indirect spiritual exchange can occur and can be a fruitful contribution for the development of the School for Spiritual Science. Now we send our good wishes to you for all circumstances and for great strength in mastering your life situation.
>
> With warmest greetings, also from our other colleagues in the Executive Council.

To conclude this contribution, I would like to quote from my address at the Annual General Meeting on 22 March, 2013:

> Since Rudolf Steiner's death no one who was active in the Executive Council had to step back due to illness. Sergei Prokofieff has now had to withdraw due to health reasons, as he wrote in his letter in *Anthroposophy Worldwide*, Nr. 1-2, 2013. His withdrawal, spiritually speaking, does not change anything for him, because he is still in the stream of continuity of the Executive Council, even if he cannot carry the task as earlier.
>
> I want to express merely a simple word of gratitude. I am saying 'simple', because that is Sergei Prokofieff's wish. We know that at the Annual General Meeting 2011 Sergei Prokofieff was affirmed in his work by a great majority of the members present. We always rejoiced when we had word from him through Seija Zimmermann. Even with all of the 'ups and downs' we expected that he could rejoin us in the Executive Council. At the end of October we had a conversation with him, which also included the members of the 'extended Council', who were three General Secretaries at that time: Ron Dunselman (Holland), Hartwig Schiller (Germany) and Marc Desaules (Switzerland), as well as Peter Selg. It was a significant occasion because we could hear from Sergei Prokofieff aspects which could be improved. We wanted to speak with him about these matters again, but it could not happen. In a conversation with him in November we experienced again his patience in regard to his condition. Then in January 2013, he informed us that due to his health situation it would not be possible for him to join us again.
>
> Sergei Prokofieff and his works are highly esteemed by thousands of people all over the world where anthroposophy has a presence. One can ask: 'What is this?' It is a phenomenon and appears for the first time in the history of this Society, that so many works from one person have been published, aside of course from Rudolf Steiner, and that they are welcomed with such enthusiasm. I have the impression

that through his own study and his exact research beginning already before his 30th year in life, that he has become ever more and more an interpreter for the works of Rudolf Steiner.

By 'interpreter' I mean someone who through his own research can recognize what radiates through Rudolf Steiner. Rudolf Steiner lived in the world of archetypal pictures. Sergei Prokofieff had the possibility to approach the reflection of these archetypes and to convey those which appear in Rudolf Steiner's works. This promotes a significant support for study. In his situation today (March 2013) Sergei Prokofieff's great hope is that he will be able to finish two books. In an initial form they are finished. He also has other plans for publications. We can all hope that this can be accomplished. We want to thank him—and probably according to his inner feeling I have already said too much—to thank him for his enormous work!

To conclude this contribution eight years after his death, I would like to express a request. When we look to the future to ten, twenty, thirty years—when perhaps most of us may not be any longer on the earth—the books by Sergei Prokofieff about Rudolf Steiner's works and his mission will be here. My request is that we do not form a 'cloud' around Sergei either through eventual criticism nor through our enthusiasm; an excessive enthusiasm can prevent some people to find an approach to him. My wish is that we direct our enthusiasm inwardly through our will to work further with anthroposophy, on the basis of the help which we received from Sergei Prokofieff.

Accompanying the feeling of our loss of him as a kind and supportive colleague, I and many other people whose impulses for the realization of anthroposophy which he also carried in his consciousness, experience him as assistance and inspiration even now after eight years.

Goetheanum, Dornach, February 2025, Virginia Sease

Elisaveta Nikolayevna Gulbina

Memories of Sergei Prokofieff

My first meeting with Sergei came about at the Michaelmas conference in 1988, which took place in Moscow for the first time since the closing of the Anthroposophical Society in Russia in 1923.

It is difficult to describe the enthusiasm which was present at all the meetings in various places in the city. At that time Sergei gave lectures about the Archangel Michael, about Rudolf Steiner's addresses to Russians in 1912 and 1913 in Helsinki, where the Doctor implanted the first shoots of the Russian Anthroposophical Society in the souls of the Russian friends assembled around him. And it was these shoots of the future Anthroposophical Society in Russia that Sergei Prokofieff communicated to us.

He was a true representative of anthroposophy in Russia on the world stage, and also a true son of his people. This was expressed in his whole outward appearance, in his nobility and exalted nature but also in his character. I have never met a person in whom brilliant abilities and spiritual power were combined with a remarkable modesty and simplicity. I never heard Sergei censuring another person, speaking scornfully about someone or expressing any kind of mockery of another human being, even when those around him were indulging in such behaviour.

Russians have the important faculty of attending not only to what is said but above all to how it is said. Sergei always spoke of the spirit, of high spiritual things, in such a way that one felt that what he was saying is true inasmuch as the person who had said it was in harmony with this truth.

Perhaps I am idealizing my picture of Sergei, but the fact was that when I was in personal contact with him I was always presented with his soul-spiritual essence, and this determined the character of our friendship. I always felt that an individuality of the highest order was before me, and my attitude towards this individuality was always filled with inner reverence.

I once shared my experiences regarding my spiritual friend with Annie Jahn, a remarkable anthroposophist who had long been friendly with Sergei and had supported his work and his lecturing activity. She was the first emissary of the world Anthroposophical Society who consciously sought meetings with Russian anthroposophists in the years of the Soviet dictatorship. Annie Jahn highly valued Sergei, and saw in him the hope of anthroposophy not only in Russia but in the whole world. She also possessed a clairvoyant gift. Once, when I was staying with her in a little village in the Swiss mountains, we had a conversation about Russia, about its destiny, about the knights of the spirit in our time; and then she shared with me her spiritual experience about representatives of our people, naming Sergei and Alexei Zhukov. Behind Sergei, she said, there appears the individuality of Christian Rosenkreutz, although she was thinking not of an incarnation of this individuality but of an incorporation. This completely corresponded with my personal experience in regard to our friend.

As for Alexei Zhukov, she informed me that her spiritual experience spoke of his connection with Ludwig II of Bavaria. Alexei himself confirmed this experience of hers also to me, in answer to my question. When I was preoccupied with the theme of Ludwig II, I turned my attention to the connection of this king with Wagner. In his lectures Rudolf Steiner speaks of Wagner as being the reincarnated Merlin, the teacher and faithful counsellor of King Arthur. In the nineteenth century this connection has the reverse character: now Arthur serves the former Merlin, and this means that we can suggest a connection of Ludwig II with Arthur.

I recall a story that Alexei Zhukov told about his childhood. It turns out that as a child he lived in the same part of Moscow as Sergei, not far from the metro station Novoslobodskaya, on Miussky ulitsa (street). There was there a small square with a children's playground, where little Alyosha played and met with little Sergei. They befriended one another, and Alexei related that Sophia Leonidovna, Sergei's mother, told him and also the other children the stories of the Knights of King Arthur. As Alyosha later joked, he came to know Sergei in a sandpit. It should be said that in my pedagogical activity I have often turned to the stories that Sophia Leonidovna Prokofieva told about the knights and always observed her deep interest in this theme which is of such importance for esoteric Christianity. I then often inwardly pondered this picture of two boys playing together, two knights of the spirit in the past and in the future.

Sergei Prokofieff had a great influence on my spiritual development: his books *The Spiritual Origins of Eastern Europe and the Future Mysteries of the Holy Grail*, *The Riddle of Dmitri* and *The Occult Significance of Forgiveness* became for me the foundations of my own creative spiritual work and of my lecturing activity on the themes of Russian history. Especially the 'Grail mood' led me to Lake Svetloyar: I was interested in the connection of the City of Kitezh with the legends about the Grail in Western Europe. In this remarkable region beyond the Volga there still live to this day spiritual verses of Old Believers about 'The Book of the Doves' and about Prester John. A group of anthroposophists from Moscow and Nizhni Novgorod has for 15 years been giving seminars on Lake Svetloyar, at the foundation of which are themes such as 'The Holy Grail of Western and Eastern Europe', 'The Riddles of Russian and World History', 'Rosicrucianism in Russia', 'Europe as a Single Organism'. Within the framework of the seminars there are always studies on the forms of the first Goetheanum: modelling of the capitals, architraves, models of the building. Sergei with Astrid and Ursula Preuss, the translator of his books into German, visited these places on Lake Svetloyar. As we also did, Sergei posed the question about the existence of the City of Kitezh, which according to the legend lies at the bottom of the lake. But quite independently of what is affirmed by this legend he always felt that this is one of the spiritual centres leading to Shamballa, where the Holy Grail is still preserved.

Sergei at home, 2011

After Sergei had left the physical plane I sorely experienced this loss, but I can say that he is alive and is helping us very actively. I have been given the great consolation of experiencing the individuality of Sergei after he crossed the threshold of the spiritual world. He appeared before me as young, spirit-filled and beautiful and said that he is alive and that I should communicate this to others. Thus he has remained for me living, active and helpful just as he always helped us during life.

Rolf Herzog

Life Encounters

The arc spanning my memories of Sergei Prokofieff extends from the first lecture that he gave in January 1982 in the great hall of the Stuttgart Waldorf School on Haussmannstrasse until he crossed the threshold of death. Shortly before this it was, after intimate, intensive conversations and meetings had preceded it, granted to me to give him the last anointing.

My first impression at the lecture was that a person was speaking out of his innermost being, out of his individual connection with the divine-spiritual world, in ardent veneration for Rudolf Steiner. I experienced every word as truthful, clear, inwardly fulfilled and experienced, authentic. All my subsequent encounters strengthened this impression. In the years of his membership of the Vorstand at the Goetheanum, these encounters were—through my priestly responsibilities in the Basel parish of The Christian Community—ever and again characterized by mutual trust and respect for the tasks of the other. I experienced him during lectures and conferences at the Goetheanum, where I was often also involved, also in the Paracelsus branch in Basel, in the context of the School of Spiritual Science with read and freely held Class Lessons, at numerous funerals in which he participated.

During the time of his illness I was astonished how he viewed his path of destiny and could accept the sorrow and pain that it brought as something belonging to himself wholly out of the spirit. He endeavoured to be someone who was always learning, one who sought and asked, a person of modesty. 'Go through your Golgotha' was the cry that he had heard in the Easter days of 2011. The constant mystery-secret of 'dying and becoming' belonged and corresponded wholly to his being.

After the appearance of his book *The First Class of the Michael School and its Christological Foundations*, I asked him how he was able to write such a book with all these connections and contents. He said that the writing was not really the problem; the question was, rather, how people can read and work with it. I experienced the immense gratitude and quiet joy with which he wrote the second volume entitled *The Esoteric Path through the Nineteen Class Lessons*. It was concerned wholly with the Christ with whom he felt connected to the extent that his memories extended and whom he had wanted to serve from his early years. Thus he had asked himself the question whether he might become a priest of the Orthodox Church, which to be sure did not seem possible. Later, when he was asked to translate the sacraments of The Christian Community as renewed by Rudolf Steiner into Russian, the question of the calling to become a priest resurfaced and was answered without further ado that his life's work lay within spiritual science. He sought to fulfil it with strict discipline and with the greatest claims upon himself and his fellow human beings, always in the hope of being able to stand before Rudolf Steiner. His evenings marking the days of Rudolf Steiner's birth and death were always special moments. One could be astonished with every year at what shone forth before his inner eye and with what devotion and dedication he spoke, how livingly and vividly Rudolf Steiner could be experienced.

His path of life stood in the sign of the three mysteries of the present: of Michael, of Chirst and of evil.[15] He was someone who entered fully into these themes and challenges; he identified himself with the task of being a representative of the Anthroposophical Society. One always breathed a high spiritual air in his presence and experienced him as having deepest reverence and gratitude for the life's work of Rudolf Steiner. At one level everything was familiar and known to him. Through his extensive study of the writings and lectures he was able to take everything into his own thoughts and form his life accordingly.

---

[15]Rudolf Steiner, lecture of 12 September 1924, *The Book of Revelation and the Task of the Priest* (GA 346).

He experienced his endeavours within the Vorstand from 2001 to 2011 against the background of the first century that had elapsed after the end of the Kali Yuga. Rudolf Steiner had drawn attention to this span of time:[16] 'Humanity will either stand at the grave of all civilization or at the beginning of that age when Michael's battle on behalf of his impulse will be fought out in the souls of those human beings who in their hearts unite intelligence and spirituality.' He involved himself in this with all his strength and tried to inspire people to kindle in their souls a Whitsun fire. His speech and the content of his lectures were full of deep seriousness and responsibility, as were the written words of his books. He suffered constantly, because much was not, and could not be, in accordance with his ideals, ideas, aims and his essential being. But he was always able to develop vanquishing forces from the spiritual aims living within him. Through painful renunciation he experienced how the inner power that overcomes all resistance—divine, creative love—is intensified and deepened. It became for him the foundation of his ceaseless quest for higher knowledge, for HIM who is the way, the truth and the life.

Ulrike Drew

Motzstraβe Berlin

I always had the impression that Sergei Prokofieff already knew, had already cultivated and integrated anthroposophy before he encountered it in this life. I shall therefore relate an experience, a brief moment, with him that strengthened this impression.

It was in the spring of 1996. Sergei had come to Berlin for several lectures and was during this week a guest in our family. On the last day of his stay he had resolved to go to the Motzstraβe and visit the place of Rudolf Steiner's activities there. I went there with him together with my little eighteen-month-old daughter. We had not long been living in Berlin and I did not myself as yet know the relevant places in the Motzstraβe.

I shall never forget with what holy reverence he entered the block of rented flats in the backyard. We then went up by the stairwell in order

[16]Lecture of 19 July 1924 in *Karmic Relationships*, Vol. VI, GA 240.

to look for the door of Rudolf Steiner's former flat. Sergei was very quiet. Very slowly, both inwardly and outwardly focussed, he climbed the stairs step by step, his hand on the banister, touching it only very lightly, until we came to a front door before which he stopped. I do not know whether it was the right door; there was no plaque, no indication of Rudolf Steiner's life here.

We stopped here for a long time with rapt attention. Also my little daughter Maria, who had hitherto been happily surmounting the steps, kept inwardly still. At this moment it seemed to me as if he was completely internalizing this situation, as if he were looking within for clues, for spirit-remembering. It was in any case a moment of deep reverence which made his true veneration for Rudolf Steiner discernible. His whole contemplative soul-power could be experienced then, even by the little child at his feet.

Astrid Prokofieff

A visit to India and a conversation with Dilnawaz and Aban Bana

The two sisters Dilnawaz and Aban Bana came to know Sergei in December 1981 in connection with his lectures in Dornach in the student house. Annie Jahn drew their attention to these lectures; and Uta Heck, who came from London and had met Sergei in London in the autumn of 1981, spread the news of the visit of this young Russian to Dornach. A further lecture was announced to take place in the student house in January 1982. But when Rudolf Grosse saw how people were coming in large numbers, everyone moved from the student house to the Grundsteinsaal (the foundation stone hall). How the elderly ladies hurried down the path to the Goetheanum in order to get a good place in the hall! But the Groundsteinsaal was also quickly full. Then Rudolf Grosse stood up and declared with a powerful voice: 'This won't work here, let's go up to the great hall.' Again everyone got up and arrived late, but Sergei O. Prokofieff's lecture began in a full hall from a small lectern. With a clear voice and yet moved by the unexpected destiny of speaking in this place, he began delivering his lecture.

Aban shared with her sister what she recognized in Sergei O. Prokofieff: 'This is a spiritual human being such as one seldom meets. He has so much light.'

His presence was always filled with good thoughts; he wasted no sad thoughts about the situation in the Soviet Union. The two sisters asked for a short meeting with Sergei in order to express their thanks before they were to travel to India for ever. They were able to shake hands with Sergei and took this encounter with them to India as a message that there are spiritual personalities also in Europe. They knew such people in India.

Subsequently, a journey to India was arranged together with invitations to Australia, New Zealand, the Philippines and Japan. This became possible in August/September 1997. Sergei and Astrid undertook this special journey together. Aban met us in Mumbai at the airport, and we went by taxi past the slums that were very close to the road to the private quarters of a relative, the Marfatia family. Mr Marfatia is very cultured and open-minded, loves European classical and modern music. There was a piano, unfortunately with many shortcomings; and it hadn't been tuned for a long time. Nevertheless, Astrid was able to practise on it.

Sergei O. Prokofieff had been asked to give a lecture about the biography of the composer Sergei S. Prokofiev, his grandfather, with little musical interludes from Astrid on the piano. It took place in a hall of the National Theatre, with a concluding discussion on various themes and a grand-scale reception in the private villa of Mrs Misteri. Even in tropical India, Sergei always had a spruce appearance, a suit and a tie. His way of speaking, his 'regal' choice of words, are an example for young people.

A further task that was important for Sergei was a lecture at the 'K.R. Cama Oriental Institute', where a meeting took place with scholars and Parsees, that is, followers of Zoroastrianism, the Zarathustra religion. Sergei spoke about the appreciation extended to Zarathustra in the West through anthroposophy and early medieval spiritual streams. Naturally, there were very divergent views among the many listeners. Aban Bana had herself been born into this religion together with her family.

There followed visits at the initiative of the Trida Waldorf School and the street children initiative, where Aban Bana taught. A further visit was made to the shrine of the Parsees in Udvada, where Aban occupied a small dwelling. There were also many meetings with priests and scholars in Hindu temples and an exchange with a group of professors and spiritual teachers, and—by no means last—an acquaintance was made with Aban's family, her parents and brother together with his wife. They had an Anglo-Indian education and culture. Her father had been a factory owner, and he had an openness towards anthroposophy and European culture. We travelled on foot, by train, bus, hitchhiking and rickshaw and thus experienced the country and its people.

Years later a chance meeting took place with Aban in the metro in Moscow, where Sergei, Karla Kiniger and I were staying for courses in the Anthroposophical Society, whereas Aban was visiting the city for a few days on her way back from India to Switzerland. We arranged to have tea with Sergei's mother. Since then Aban has sent her greetings to her.

Sergei during his lecture at the Cama Oriental Institute, 1997

In the 1990s and 2000s Aban, sometimes also together with Dilnawaz, met Sergei in Dornach at conferences or during the annual meetings of the country representatives of the Anthroposophical Society at the Goetheanum. These were always happy and warm-hearted reunions. A last visit took place in 2014 shortly before Sergei's death. Aban wanted to bring only greetings and warm wishes, but having been asked Sergei wanted a short meeting. He lay in his bed, and was very weak. He said: 'I must diminish, He must increase.' Aban was deeply shocked. She had not seen Sergei for several years and needed the consolation of Astrid. Aban said that she could experience his full spirituality. She was at the funeral in Dornach during the conference of the School of Spiritual Science at the Goetheanum.

Sandip Kamad, a master of biodynamics in India, as Aban called him, said on hearing the news of Sergei's death: 'It has been an important time for us to have had Sergei on Earth, for him to have been active in Dornach and working in the Vorstand. A spiritual human being!' Dilnawaz and Aban wholly concurred with these words.

Oliviera Todorovic

Sergei Prokofieff in Belgrade

In the year 2005 I took six friends from Belgrade to the Anthroposophical Society 'Maria Sophia' in Zagreb. This was the first meeting of anthroposophists from Serbia with those from Croatia and Slovenia after the war, after December 1991. The occasion of the journey was that of the visit of Sergei Prokofieff organized by the Zagreb Society and his lecture about the First Class. The anthroposophists from Serbia were strongly impressed by the fact that at last someone from the Slavic regions had become a member of the Vorstand of the General Anthroposophical Society. On the morning of this day, Sergei Prokofieff allotted one or two hours just for the friends from Serbia. At that time we were not yet conscious of his personal stature. During this meeting in Zagreb it was also agreed that he would visit Belgrade. This came about in 2007 during his journey through the Balkan lands. On 20 and 21 June 2007 he gave two lectures for a small group of around 20 listeners. The lecture was as usual given in German, but after a pause Prokofieff continued in Russian; he spontaneously felt the wish to speak before this audience in his mother tongue.

There is one anecdote that we all remember. When Prokofieff was with us it was very hot in Belgrade, between 35 and 40 C. Together with our guest we were visiting the Botanical Garden and also the tropical house as part of the garden. He went with some friends into the tropical house, while the others remained outside totally exhausted by the heat. After a while two of the friends came out, since they couldn't bear the heat. When the visit was over, Sergei Prokofieff and his companion emerged. One could see that he was not unduly troubled, whereas his companion stood beside him dripping with sweat. This scene was unforgettable for us.

Van James

A Recollection of Sergei Prokofieff

I first met Sergei Prokofieff in 1979 at a small gathering of mostly American faculty members of Emerson College in the home of John Davy in Forest Row, England (Anne Stockton and John Meeks were present, among others). It was Sergei's first time out of Russia and John Davy, O.B.E., the co-director of Emerson College at the time, had invited him to speak about his experiences of studying anthroposophy under the trying conditions in the Soviet Union. A former science correspondent for the *Observer,* John also wanted to encourage a Russian-American, East-West conversation.

I was 30 years old and teaching at the newly founded Tobias School of Art. Sergei was 26 with very basic but adequate English-speaking skills. He described the secret anthroposophical gatherings in his homeland, the tension of being under surveillance, and the selection of topics which members of the group would prepare and lecture on to the others in the group. It painted a very striking picture and a distinct contrast to the way study groups met with ease in the West.

John Davy asked if I could walk Sergei up to Tobias the next day and give him a tour of the cottage-like art studios above the village of Forest Row. We walked over the rolling green hills of the golf course at the edge of Ashdown Forest and Sergei commented on what a peaceful dream-like feeling the verdant English landscape presented. He described how different it was from his homeland where one was inclined to want to sit down and ponder the landscape in order to be present in it. I told him how in America, my homeland, one felt driven to engage one's will by moving through the landscape in order to experience it. Our conversation concerning East and West that day was very stimulating and it was a theme we would pick up together later in our lives. At Tobias School of Art, Sergei showed a fascination for my early neo-surrealist paintings, more so than the current work done in an anthroposophical style. As a former art student himself, he expressed great interest in the artistic trends and styles current in the West.

Years later, after many books were written, lectures were delivered and travels were made on both our parts, Sergei found his way to Hawaii where I had settled. He demonstrated through his conversations and lectures his now deeply mature grasp of anthroposophy and Christology. His powerful connection to the Foundation Stone Meditation, the School of Spiritual Science and the Michael Impulse was remarkably formed and articulated.

However, one of my most memorable experiences with Sergei was taking him around the island of O'ahu and introducing him to the ancient cultural sites of Hawaii. By now he had experienced the North American continent and its strong north-south magnetic mountain ranges, not to mention many other parts of the world. But here in the mid-Pacific was a different convergence of geographic and life forces that were new to him. He was especially sensitive to the ancient atavistic energies that still reside in some of the places we visited. Yet, he seemed most taken and deeply refreshed by a swim in the gentle and healing, yet awesomely powerful, Pacific Ocean. He did not want to shower after his swim so that he could have the sea salt remain on his skin for the rest of the day (something he made a point of expressing), and it made me think of the subsurface sandy, salt deposits of Russia that encourage one to sit down and take in the nature of that part of the world. Sergei Prokofieff was a Michaelic Citizen of the world and yet, at the same time, a true representative of the land of the sixth cultural epoch.

The last time I saw Sergei was at the Goetheanum, where he had eventually made his home-away-from-home as a member of the Executive Council there. When left to his thoughts, Sergei's countenance expressed the weight of the world, the deep suffering of his Slavic destiny, and his own melancholic temperament. But when Sergei made eye contact his face lit up and glowed with the radiance of the sun.

Barbara Mraz

Companionship in Life

I no longer know when I heard of Sergei Prokofieff for the first time in my life; it was during my time in the upper school in the late 1980s. I had often heard his name from several of the teachers who accompanied me and fostered my abilities during my schooldays at the Hamburg-Wandsbek Rudolf Steiner School. My father also frequently mentioned him in his conversations with a very old anthroposophist whom we regularly visited as a family.

These conversations fell during the time of my decision to make my deep love for eurythmy, which had until this time been my great secret, openly apparent and that I would take up eurythmy as my destiny task and profession. For several of the people around me, this seemed a strange thing to do and it provoked considerable resistance.

I already had a great interest and a quite natural love for Russian culture and art, a deep longing to meet people from this nation and a quiet hope that I might be able to pursue a task in that country. So I was always wide awake and full of interest when I heard something of Sergei Prokofieff, his destiny and his being and work.

In 1991, right at the beginning of my eurythmy studies in Hamburg, I met him for the first time. Carina Schmidt had invited him to speak about Rudolf Steiner's path of life and his destiny-task, quite in general but also with regard to eurythmy. I had a particular idea of this person and I was very excited to discover what my first personal impression would be. My greatest surprise was that he was much younger than I had estimated after everything that I had heard of him. He entered the room in which the whole eurythmy school was gathered (at the time about 85 people) almost shyly. An upright, tall, thin figure stood before us with a very serious, pale countenance and an unruly strand of hair that stood out from the back of his head. He began to speak with a full, deep voice and an unmistakable Russian accent, quite shyly to start with; one sensed that it was not every day that he had to speak to so many students who did not know much about the personality of Rudolf Steiner. But once he had begun, one could tell how surely he was inwardly at home in what he had undertaken to say to us. It seemed to me as if he inwardly had a whole panorama in his mind from which he could speak quite impressively without any outward support and answer the students' questions; it was as though Rudolf Steiner's personality was an immediate presence to him out of which he was able to speak. An unshakable love and a genuine power of enthusiasm streamed through everything that he said. One could see that he was speaking of the being and work of that person in whose service he had placed the whole of his own being. And this without any compromise. This impressed not only me but also many other students. Through Sergei Prokofieff an initial awareness arose within our student community of the high significance of Rudolf Steiner's earthly path and the whole of his creative work and how this is bound up with eurythmy.

A short time later I experienced Sergei Prokofieff again at the youth conference *'von wegen Freiheit…'* (so much for freedom…), where he again spoke about Rudolf Steiner's destiny. His concern here was with Rudolf Steiner's inner deed of transformation in view of the catastrophic burning of the first Goetheanum, the ensuing months and his free resolve not to turn away from something but to take over the chairmanship of the newly founded Society. He also focussed upon the great risk that this posed for Rudolf Steiner personally and upon what this deed means for his further destiny and what he has thereby taken upon himself.

At that time Sergei Prokofieff posed the question to us young people as to what we would then call a free destiny-task. He took Rudolf Steiner's life as an example of this. He posed the further question to us as to how we wished to relate today to this free deed, what it could mean for us with respect to the Anthroposophical Society and whether we would not see that, with everything that has lived and continues to live in the Society in all its light and shadows, Rudolf Steiner has ever since borne this karmic burden—thus whether we wanted inwardly through a free resolve to stand at his side in order to carry this, and what such a free decision would signify for our own life's destiny.

This lecture by Sergei Prokofieff fundamentally transformed my own destiny, for—wholly contrary to my intention under no circumstances to join this Society through which I had from without already experienced so much that was disappointing and which corresponded so little to my own ideals—I decided on the same evening to connect myself with the Society by joining it and, moreover, for the reason that Sergei Prokofieff had formulated and had so powerfully and clearly presented to us. It was for me like a powerful knock at the inner door of my own conscience which has to this day not been silenced, bearing in mind that the next test to be undergone is how I myself want to stand towards and within this Society. The real reason for my joining is constantly renewed in the recollection of this mighty lecture and the inner agreement that went and goes with it—to stand in a wholly modest way at Rudolf Steiner's side through one's own work and, through a free resolve of the will, to contribute one's responsibility for the wider picture, precisely because the Society is not what it could be and how I would for myself wish it to be. I subsequently learnt that other young listeners also took and implemented the same decision on this day.

A short time later, Sergei Prokofieff again came to the eurythmy school in Hamburg, but this time in order to accompany the premiere of the Hamburg eurythmy stage-group presentation entitled 'Europe and the Dignity of Man' by giving introductory lectures. On this occasion I heard him speak for the first time about the spiritual tasks of Central Europe in relation to the European East, and in connection with this about the destiny of Goethe and Schiller, the circumstances of the latter's death and about Caspar Hauser. I continued to dwell upon what he said, and the foundation was laid for subsequent personal meetings.

Eleven years later, in 2004, I came to the Goetheanum as a member of the stage-group ensemble. This was at the very time when Sergei Prokofieff was giving some remarkable lectures about Friedrich Schiller, who has been a guiding star in my life since my early youth. I still have a vivid picture of the enthusiasm with which Sergei Prokofieff spoke about the young Friedrich Schiller in the circle of his birth family. His whole face glowed radiantly when he spoke about the high idealism of this young man, when he described Schiller's physically delicate constitution, the great spirit that dwelt within it and had a life-long struggle with it, and his battle to wrest from life everything necessary for his lofty task. He spoke about the exemplary education of the will that Friedrich Schiller imposed upon himself right until his last words before crossing the threshold. He described the great capacity for love that accompanied Friedrich Schiller's ideal of freedom and how this was taken up and further developed by Rudolf Steiner in his *Philosophy of Freedom*. Through these lectures, my own youthful ideals arose within me with a new power and on a new level. The great gratitude that I felt for this enabled me to summon up the courage to speak personally to Sergei Prokofieff and to thank him for this.

With this I took up a gesture that he had extended to me in the autumn of 2004 a week after my reception in the ensemble at the Goetheanum. He came up to me after the first collegial gathering in which I had participated, took me firmly by the hand without relaxing his grasp, welcomed me very warmly and spoke to me quite directly and very seriously about the ideals that had led me to the Goetheanum and which I wanted to introduce, and also about what might possibly arise from this. He asked me for a dialogue about this, which I was, however, able to take up only after these lectures about Schiller and which then developed at increasingly regular intervals, enriched with many themes.

In 2005 I also experienced his shattering lectures about the circumstances of Friedrich Schiller's death and the connection to be discerned with the end of Rudolf Steiner's life. In listening and on further reflection there arose within me the question whether he was conscious that this hostility which he had described to me so clearly and unequivocally might also be directed against himself when he openly expressed these connections so courageously. I was able subsequently to raise and discuss this question personally with him through something that I had experienced directly. In my house there was at that time living someone who had already threatened Sergei Prokofieff. I therefore kept an eye on this person. When it became clear that an acute readiness to use force against Sergei Prokofieff had arisen in this individual through a psychic illness and that this had been proclaimed by the person concerned in my presence, I informed the police. As they did not arrive in time and this person was making his way to Sergei Prokofieff's house, I called him in order to warn him. We subsequently spoke about the actual incident. But we also spoke about his whole situation and about the forces that had already on several occasions been directed against him on many levels through different circles and personalities. I could only be astonished at his unshakable inner calm when he described the more precise circumstances, at his great trust that I would keep silent about them and at the totally matter-of-fact, completely objective way in which he spoke about this destiny-situation. I could perceive no fear or insecurity in him but only a great peace, an utterly clear inner awareness of what he stood for and what this aroused, but also a great gratitude towards those individuals who felt connected with him and who, while leaving him free, stood in friendship by his side wherever it was needed.

When I was asked by Sergei Prokofieff in 2009 to work on a prose text by Schiller before his next lectures on the great poet and dramatist and to present this before the lectures, he again took up the themes that had lived between us in 2004/5. A direct collaboration arose through and by way of Schiller's spirit.

As a eurythmist on the Goetheanum stage, I had many encounters with Sergei Prokofieff in front of, behind and on the stage and ever and again a direct collaboration. Since perhaps not so many people are able to speak about this side of his nature, I should like to add some succinct examples of events that took place from the autumn of 2004 to the summer of 2011.

It quickly became clear to me that Sergei Prokofieff had a great love for the stage and for the arts that have newly arisen from anthroposophy or have been fructified by it, since he often came behind the stage after a performance and not infrequently came directly towards me, not only thanking me for what he had just experienced but being able and wanting to describe quite special impressions which were incomparable. Or he had asked for something that he wished for, that he very much wanted to see, which he missed, either a particular work to which he had a particular connection, or there was an element of eurythmy which he quite clearly drew to my attention. Or he asked to be allowed to give a task to be worked on. Thus during these years I was often engaged in conversation with him about artistic questions.

When the new production of Rudolf Steiner's four Mystery Plays was being prepared from 2005 onwards, one could experience Sergei Prokofieff from a side that for many of us was totally unfamiliar, that called forth not only great astonishment but also brought with it many a humorous situation. Various individuals were called upon to work upon suggestions with the ensemble. The ensemble and also the artistic leaders frequently changed, so that not everyone present had and were able to have an overview of the developmental path of this work. Particular scenes were often performed to representatives of the collegium of the School and the Vorstand that had—in the sense of the new ideas and approach—already been so far developed that they could be shown. This happened for the first time in the late autumn of 2005 and was in 2007 repeated on several occasions with a new cast. At such rehearsals there were also discussions. To our great surprise we learnt on one such occasion that Sergei Prokofieff was the only one to remember that the same scenes had already been seen a year and a half before with the same eurythmy forms (although with a different cast) and were certainly not 'new', which is what they were proclaimed to be. After much joyous or critical astonishment about 'the wholly new' production, he said quite dryly in 2007: 'We've already seen this in 2005!' To the question of one of his Vorstand colleagues, who had not noticed this despite having been present, Sergei Prokofieff then responded: 'One sees this at once—if one can remember!' He was absolutely right; it was exactly so. The ensemble found it hard to keep a straight face. Sergei Prokofieff perceived this silently with a motionless expression but with humorously sparkling eyes.

We worked on content-related questions of the plays at a morning meeting of the ensemble, and some of the Vorstand members had also come for this work. We wanted to begin at eight o'clock in the morning, but as so often happens it did not start punctually. Shortly after eight o'clock a tired Sergei Prokofieff appeared, at once observing with incomparable humour: 'This is very nice to arrive late and yet not be the last.' He did not take part in the discussion; he was sitting opposite me and I had the impression that he was inwardly far away and preoccupied with other things, but the impression was deceptive. When a difference of opinion emerged among his Vorstand colleagues about the comprehension of a scene, he intervened in order to mediate and, without speaking for a long time, was able to say quite clearly to the one who could not understand the viewpoint of the other what this viewpoint was based on and to elucidate it in such a way that not only his colleague but also the ensemble understood the other person. He then asked whether we would also like to know his own view of this scene, which was indeed the case; and so he briefly and succinctly (which was not generally his way) presented what he had to say on this subject. Through his contribution everything proceeded fruitfully; and he again adopted his previous attitude of quietly listening, while seeming inwardly to be concerned with something else.

Three weeks before the opening night, I got myself into so great an inner crisis in my allotted task as the 'Guardian of the Threshold' that I was on the point of withdrawing from it. Inexplicably, Sergei Prokofieff learnt on that very day that I had left the rehearsal full of despair. The following day I found a message on the stage noticeboard that he wanted to go for a walk with me and have a conversation, and that I should call on him at home; his telephone number and a possible time to ring him were written on the little card. I had no idea what he wanted of me and I did not particularly want to phone him in this deeply troubled state. After some reflection I nevertheless phoned him; he picked up after the first ring and asked me if I would like to go at once for a walk with him. Again I had to summon up all my courage, for my inner state was visible for all to see, which to me was not right. I had hardly arrived at his front door when Sergei Prokofieff was standing with an indescribable, loving and almost fatherly gesture before me, bade me come in, let me sit down and silently and calmly looked at me for quite a while. I was very grateful to him for this. Through this shared silence, I was able to calm down to the extent of answering him when he asked me whether I might not want to tell him what was causing me to be inwardly so full of despair that I would even consider abandoning the whole thing. I accordingly described to him my great questions about myself and the questions that were living in me through the production. He listened to everything with great interest without interrupting me. When I came to the end, he asked me whether he might read something to me. When I assented to this, he went into his study, returned with a book and very calmly read me a lecture by Rudolf Steiner. This lecture was concerned with precisely the questions that were causing me such trouble at the time, and some highly significant thoughts about the nature of the Guardian of the Threshold and his task were addressed which again gave me a foundation; and I could continue to work with my own questions and in such a way that they were able to flow fruitfully into the eurythmy form, thus giving me an inner sense of direction for my further development. The conversation which Sergei Prokofieff subsequently had with me was like speaking with an artistic colleague. He was indeed an artist who himself knew all the heights and depths of an artistic soul and had himself experienced them. Moreover, he discussed with me what this task of being allowed to represent the Guardian of the Threshold signifies biographically for the exponent and on what he or she could inwardly work. The whole conversation took its course in such a way that with every new step he asked me whether I wanted to share this with him; and it was only once I had given my agreement that he continued to speak or posed the next question. I can hardly recall another conversation of so decisive a nature where I was left so free and yet received such loving, practical help as this indeed was. I returned home totally transformed, inwardly encouraged and with a new sense of affirmation towards my task, and was able to begin anew the following day.

I asked Sergei Prokofieff in conclusion to give me a clear reflection after the premiere of what he would perceive in my performance, so that I could work further on it. He refused, since he did not have sufficient awareness of eurythmy to be a competent conversation partner. I therefore asked him to look at my performance as an anthroposophist—with this he was in agreement.

At the festive gathering after the opening night he came up to me and asked for a conversation in private. What now happened is unique in my professional biography until now, for he described in detail scene by scene, speech by speech and sometimes even precise moments during speeches what he had seen and perceived and how this was to be viewed in harmony (or also not) with what he had derived and further developed from anthroposophy with regard to the nature of the Guardian. And not only that—he discussed in every detail all eurythmical means that I had employed; he knew from a single seeing exactly which speech I had worked out the details of and he also saw quite clearly which inner motives had led me to this. He clearly remembered when I took a step forwards, when I had taken some backwards and why and where I had interspersed quite gentle eurythmy forms into the long periods of standing. Neither before nor since have I ever received such an exact reflection, whether from a colleague or from any other person. It was full of warmth and deep respect for the individuality standing before him and for her artistic freedom. He addressed this consciously and strengthened it through the perceptions that he described. He visibly enjoyed this dialogue and that I could experience my actions as in a mirror in his description. It was similar to Schiller's first letter to Goethe: one has to speak *out of* the mind that one contemplates and not *about* it. For me it was a special hour of destiny that lives on and is ever present.

Sergei Prokofieff was often to be met with behind the stage; he liked to speak of his childhood and how through his beloved grandmother he associated with the artistic circles of Moscow and sat beside her on a little chair that she kept by for him when she conversed with the artists after performances, and how greatly he loved this atmosphere. Shortly before the start of a performance, he liked to go across the south stage into the hall, looked briefly through the doors where the stage manager was at the stage, wished us all the best and exchanged a glance with the performers.

One could occasionally also meet him in the costume department, where he liked to have a cup of tea. One day, with many humorous remarks, he devotedly organized and sorted all the buttons into the little drawers intended for them. While doing so he also with great delight related to me a memory of his governess or 'nanny'.

One morning he appeared unusually early in the performers' cafe behind the stage; one could see at once that this was not his favourite time of day. He came up to me with weary steps and wanted to invite me for a coffee. When I tried to break it gently to him that I would very much like to sit down with him but do not drink coffee, he jerked himself awake and wanted desperately to know from me 'How do you do such a thing and still manage to live...?'; and he broke out into sympathetic laughter and drank his beloved coffee with visible pleasure, happy to see that there was also a sweet cake in front of him and smiling to himself quite contentedly.

In 2009 I spoke with Sergei Prokofieff in order to ask him for help and support for a combined guest performance of the Goetheanum stage-group and the Else Klink ensemble in Moscow with the last of the three eurythmy symphony projects. He agreed immediately and made some helpful suggestions. I knew that he had his reservations about the contemporary music that we often included in our various programmes. We also wanted to perform such a work in Moscow. I asked him whether his support would be possible in spite of his reservations. He was surprised at my question, looked at me quite openly and said: 'I can perfectly well distinguish between music for which I personally have reservations and excellent eurythmy which I want to promote. I shall fully support you! As artists you are always free, also in your own artistic decisions, you must do what you have in mind to do. We do not need to share the same preferences.' We went to Moscow with the planned programme and had his full backing.

A shared rehearsal on the Foundation Stone Meditation with Sergei Prokofieff was especially impressive. He worked thoroughly through the demonstration that he had asked of us for a lecture, and explained precisely with the relevant background material why it was as it was and not otherwise. When we again wanted to present the Foundation Stone Meditation, Carina Schmidt asked him to speak the verse for us as he himself related to it, which he then did after some hesitation. We formed the verse together with him. It was a great joy and at the same time a challenge, especially in the quick forms of the macrocosmic parts of the verse. His inner love and his inner work on the mantra were so present and inwardly moving in his speech that the eurythmy movements could find an immediate connection with the way he spoke. In the forming and above all in the anticipation of every gesture, one had to find the highest presence of mind, since there was much that was unfamiliar to us in the way he expressed or emphasized it. But through his involvement it directly irradiated the movement itself. After this experience, his written explanations opened up to me a deepened insight. The way he spoke the mantra continues to resound for me to this day as I work with it.

When in 2010 it became clear that through the change of the stage leadership my task at the Goetheanum would come to an end, a new side of Sergei Prokofieff came to show itself. The time of the decision as to who out of the members of the ensemble would form part of the stage-group fell during the last performances of the Mystery Plays before the summer break. When on the day of the third play I arrived backstage in order to prepare myself for the first entrance, I learnt from colleagues that Sergei Prokofieff was looking for me in every interval and had asked them to inform me of this. I therefore met him in the next interval. He asked me to go with him to a place where we could speak without being disturbed. One could see that he was inwardly very emotional and had something on his mind. I did not have much time until my entrance and would also have liked to be alone. He sensed how I felt and wanted to advise me how I might manage things in the moment of performance and how he would inwardly help to carry the situation. The inner sharing of the load was not only clearly perceptible and a help but he also came behind the stage in every further interval, also on the following day, in order to convince himself that everything was in order. Already during the applause at the end of the fourth play it was clear who—like myself—would leave the Goetheanum after a year. He came behind the stage again and asked for a further conversation in private. He spoke so directly and openly, as I had not previously experienced him to do, about where he saw my future tasks and how he had to conduct himself in a comparable moment and was therefore obliged and enabled to undergo a painful but very rich time of maturation on a distinctive path of his own. He gave me much requisite insight as an inner help for this path, so that I had a year in order to prepare myself before my life's path led me away from the Goetheanum. During these days he was someone manifesting his full humanity, fatherly, very loving, with a great Russian sympathetic heart and sharing everything in a real way. He said what he thought about the whole situation then at the Goetheanum, how he experienced it personally but also in relation to myself. He did not stab anyone in the back and stood by his own responsibility in a realm beyond the personal. Nevertheless in what he said about the structures at the Goetheanum and about relations with fellow human beings in such a situation, there was no lack of clarity. I share all this not in the interests of my personal situation but in order to make it clear that the assertion that I often hear, that Sergei Prokofieff had few or no social abilities in his dealings with others, is totally unjustified.

During the Annual General Meeting in 2011 I came behind the stage before the remembering of the dead; everything was in darkness and the stage manager was not yet present, but I immediately felt that I was not alone; and when I looked carefully to see who was there I saw it was Sergei Prokofieff. He had withdrawn there after the day's exertions. I observed that he wasn't well and offered him my help. A deep inner sorrow then broke forth from him regarding what had taken place during the General Meeting. I was shocked to hear what he said. The next morning I met him again behind the stage in quite a different mood. He had already been waiting for me with a Vorstand colleague and wanted to know whether, firstly, I had no eurythmy shoes in the presentation during the remembrance of the dead and had performed in my stockings, and whether what I had expressed through my feet in the tone eurythmy had been the eurythmy leg intervals or had been borrowed from dance. When I confirmed to him both that I was in stockings and that I was employing the leg intervals, he laughed out loud and beamed at both his colleague and me. He said with laughter: 'Then I have won the bet!', and added somewhat roguishly: 'Now you know what kind of questions we had at the end of the General Meeting', and rejoiced mischievously about my great relief after my experience the previous evening of seeing him standing before me so utterly transformed.

In the autumn of 2007 I was unexpectedly given the task of portraying 'Michael' in the eurythmy forms that Rudolf Steiner created for the 'Michael imagination' from his last address. Through this task a new phase opened up in my eurythmy biography and it has become a quite central aspect of it. From the start I asked Sergei Prokofieff for a personal conversation. There then began a direct collaboration which ended only with his death. He suggested to me that he would continue to help me with everything that he had hitherto discerned in this mantra, but I should first please show him what I had worked out through eurythmy. He was completely open—almost with a childlike joy of discovery—to the modest beginnings that I had made by then with this last great assignment that Rudolf Steiner has entrusted to eurythmy. When I posed my crucial question, he was silent for a long time and quietly listened to his inner voice. Then he raised his head, looked firmly in my eyes and acknowledged to me how justified and important this question was but confessed it was one that he had not himself hitherto had. In order to arrive at an answer to this question, he would have to meditate about it for a long time, whereas I would have eurythmy to help me with it. He gave me the courage to approach this question through eurythmy itself. With this he took up something that Rudolf Steiner had entrusted to Ilona Schubert when she had turned to him with a related question. This was the beginning of a long path which was accompanied by Sergei Prokofieff with devoted interest, initially personally and in the time of his illness by way of his wife and a mutual female friend. In February 2011 I gave a lecture at the Goetheanum about my research questions on the Michael imagination. To my surprise and also consternation Sergei Prokofieff appeared shortly before the beginning and sat down in the front row. One could clearly see how exhausted he was. He explained to me that he wanted to support me and had therefore left the Vorstand meeting early.

In his own lecture about the Michael imagination in May 2011, one could clearly see the severity of his illness. I wondered as he spoke whether I was experiencing him directly for the last time. His lecture had the quality of a last testament not only with respect to Rudolf Steiner's Last Address but also for his own work. At the end of his mighty presentation I went up to him in order to thank him. He held my hand firmly for a long time and looked me in the eyes without speaking. Afterwards he asked me to wipe off his blackboard drawing for him, nothing should be left on the blackboard. So I stood before the eurythmy form that Rudolf Steiner gave for the silent prelude to the Michael imagination and which Sergei Prokofieff had drawn on the blackboard during the lecture in big, bold strokes.

The day before he crossed the threshold, he informed me that I should not get myself a copy of his new book *The Michael Imagination*. I found it in my letter box in Berlin with a dedication when I returned from the conference of the School of Spiritual Science and the memorial ceremony that followed in those days.

After this a new task in life was inaugurated, in that a little group of eurythmists from Moscow came to Berlin in order to become familiar with and absorb the new eurythmy impulse that has found a new home and place of work there in the last few years. Through this meeting a collaboration arose which has led me to go several times to Moscow, where I have been able to explore the Michael imagination (among other things) from anthroposophical foundations with the colleagues living there. I have come to experience in this combined work who the good spirit is who promotes it so fruitfully and, as a godfather, accompanies the many friendships that have arisen in this work—Sergei Prokofieff is the good spirit who helps in a very real way from the other side. This shows itself in many ways and fills the friends in Moscow and me with great gratitude.

Fabio Montelatici

Life Encounters

The meetings with S.O. Prokofieff stand in my biography as one of the most important 'human' encounters of my life. Also if I knew S. Prokofieff from his books, with great admiration, I saw him for the first time at the Goetheanum, during the Mystery Drama festival in 2010. He was sitting in the first rows with the other members of the Vorstand. And there I saw the first hint of the 'man', and not the 'writer'.

At the end of each pause, in that festival, there was a really old lady in the audience who took a long time to stand up and exit the room. She was always dressed in white. On the second day, in the middle of the second drama, at the beginning of an afternoon break the old lady was particularly slow to stand up and walk towards the door. Maybe she was in pain, or tired. There were 1000 people in the room, and we had all noticed the lady, but we didn't know her, and maybe for that reason nobody ever got there to help her. But in that pause, when she was slower than usual, S. Prokofieff stopped and turned towards her. He took leave of his colleagues, almost jumped over two rows of seats of the Great Hall and got to the lady. He offered her his arm and they walked together outside, speaking and smiling. You know, he was one of the 'authorities'; it wasn't his 'duty' to do something like that. But he did, and showed that he didn't consider himself an 'authority'. In the following days, one could see S. Prokofieff speaking with visitors and tourists (who probably didn't even know who he was) and showing them particular places in the Goetheanum—because he loved the Goetheanum, and loved to share this love with people, to make them 'meet' that unique place.

After that I had the gift to meet S. Prokofieff personally, in private dialogues, a couple of times. At that time I had founded a branch of the Anthroposophical Society in Italy, and this branch was in the middle of a complex opposition from other Italian members (for reasons here not relevant, and later solved). I was introduced to S. Prokofieff by a friend in Dornach, Clothilde Bernhard, who taught me that he was really helpful in these kinds of matters. And he really was. I could talk to him in his study—under the immense reproduction of Steiner's *Golgotha* and in front of the pictures of the first Vorstand—and he listened to my story with the deepest participation, showing real 'human interest' in my anthroposophical work, in my personal biography, in the understanding of my deepest concerns and ideals. He wanted to get to my 'human' core, in the heart of my being, without stopping at the surface. He was really interested also in my books, something that I found really quite strange. And there he could understand what was happening, and in the following months help to solve the oppositions created in the Italian Society. He really cared about the health of the Society, and worked actively to restore the dialogue and let us talk, meet and understand each other.

He never used his 'authority' as a famous lecturer, writer, or member of the Vorstand; he simply showed us the way to meet, to build in the name of anthroposophy and of the direction established with the Christmas Conference. I met him in Italy some time later (March 2011) and had the chance to introduce him to all the members of my branch, which he met with deep warmth.

Then he got ill, and I decided not to bother him anymore because I considered my 'story' not so important for someone like him. So it was a real surprise when, during the Italian Bologna Conference in 2011 (which I couldn't attend for practical problems), I received a phone call from the Conference asking if *I was at the Conference, because Sergei Prokofieff wished to meet me and talk with me.* That was astonishing. In the middle of this great cultural event, Sergei Prokofleff not only remembered me, but had hoped to meet me, because, I can tell from what was said in that phone call, he cared for me as a person, for me as an anthroposophist and disciple of Rudolf Steiner, and for our Society, and—last but not certainly least—for Rudolf Steiner and anthroposophy herself.

Even though I always carried in my heart the feeling to have a 'friend' at the Goetheanum, after that phone call I had no further meetings or direct contacts with S. Prokofleff. I wrote him a letter during his retirement owing to ill health, wishing him all the best and asking him not to worry about 'us', all the people who worked in the light of his and Rudolf Steiner's work. *'We are here to walk with you, not to take from you'* I wrote to him. In an unexpected meeting with Astrid Prokofleff in the Schreinerei, she said that those words were deeply appreciated.

I recall all these moments as gifts. Like with Rudolf Steiner, we can be amazed by the 'writer–lecturer', but the real substance, from whence that lecturer comes, is the man. The man is really more than

Sergei on the occasion of the Fourth International Congress for Philosophy from 31 March to 4 April 2011 in Bologna

his books or thoughts, and I am infinitely grateful to have shared some very little moments of my path with Sergei O. Prokofleff. I hope that, through my dedication to his work, we can walk together again, in a spiritual way.

Gerard Hermans

Meetings in Holland

I love Sergei, his books, his work, with all my heart. Sergei has shown that access to the source of anthroposophy is possible. I believe that even many well-respected anthroposophists often saw in him a scribe who represented an 'intellectual form' of anthroposophy, or—more formally—an 'anthroposophical hermeneutics'. I see Sergei Prokofieff's life's work as the indispensible Platonic pillar of anthroposophy.

After the last lecture at the end of a conference in Holland, the participants in the preparation group were still sitting more or less together. I was excited to be able to experience the conversation. However, I was aware of a somewhat tense atmosphere, which surprised me greatly. It gradually became clear to me that each of those present had a difficulty either with the theme of the lecture or with the way that it had been delivered or with the recognition of the personality of Sergei Prokofieff. One anthroposophist well-known in the Netherlands had directly asked Sergei in the plenum: 'How or where can the continuing working of the Christmas Conference be found today?' Sergei's answer surprised all those present, because he said: 'One should look at the eyes, at the light in people's eyes.' I think that quite a few anthroposophists were still hoping for some kind of 'culmination' of anthroposophy in the form of a social recognition. Another well-known and popular anthroposophist made it clear that he could derive no enjoyment from what was in his opinion the intellectual character of the lecture. Others related that it was easy to observe in the working groups that a deep or intimate understanding of anthroposophy was essentially lacking. Sergei suggested trying it next time with eurythmy.

For me the lectures of Sergei Prokofieff were an experience, an awakening of unexpected forces in my soul. Sergei spoke out of imaginations that he still experienced as he lectured. During a lecture he created a spiritual space in which these imaginations were present, but he himself and his listeners were also present. I have never understood why it was quite naturally possible for me to be able to be part of this space. His genuineness and his intelligent, artistic language made it possible, and the beauty and truth of these imaginations that he described went directly to my heart. It took years for me to understand that not everyone experienced his lectures like this.

I recall the way that Sergei could emphasise something important, a mystery or secret, in a lecture. In the middle of a sentence he made a little pause, a tiny moment of silence. And then the second half of the sentence was spoken seriously, with a gently resolute emphasis. I also recall the beautiful way he could inwardly laugh when—and it was mostly unexpected even for him—he subtly came up with something humorous.

He was asked in Bonn how he construed Rudolf Steiner's remark about 'the dawn of the Christian mysteries'. Christoph Lindenberg put forward a definite opinion which had given rise to discussions. Sergei began his answer with the following words: 'Our dear friend, Christoph Lindenberg'. I found it amazing that these few words defused the whole debate. Of course, his answer was also pertinent and understandable in its substance.

Simon Blaxland-de Lange

Some Reflections of a Translator

I need to start with a bit of personal background. I spent my teenage years at the height of the Cold War, and I wanted in my naïve innocence to 'do something about' this Cold War. Why should we hate the Russians? It turned out that it was possible for me to take an optional 'O' level in Russian while taking my 'A' levels, and I quickly acquired a love for this language (imparted, incidentally, by the German teacher from Austria who taught the subject) and a fascination for this culture. I should make it clear that I knew nothing about anthroposophy at this time and therefore had no awareness of what Rudolf Steiner said about the future task of the Russian people and the 'Slavic soul'. I accordingly continued my studies of Russian as part of my university degree and visited Moscow and Leningrad (as it was then) in 1970. Little did I know that there was at that time a young Russian in Moscow who was then embarking upon a remarkable series of youthful poems; while my youthful love-affair with Russia and its language would only come to further development and significance in my life when I began translating his books some time in 1986 or early 1987. This young Russian, Sergei Olegovich Prokofieff, had by 1970 already come into contact with anthroposophy; and it was during the next couple of years that I too came to know of Rudolf Steiner's work and, like Sergei, recognized it as something utterly central to my life. Since then, I have translated a considerable number of Sergei's books and lectures into English, and in reflecting upon this I have to ask myself: What is the significance of my having spent so much of my life doing this, or, to put it another way, what significance does Sergei Prokofieff's written (and spoken) work have for the English-speaking world (and for that larger circle of people who have English as their second language)?

Anthroposophy was brought by or through Rudolf Steiner into a world which, as he made very clear especially in the aftermath of the First World War, is dominated at least outwardly by a materialistic conception of man and earthly reality emanating primarily from that land that has the particular task of developing the consciousness or spiritual soul; and, as Owen Barfield has very lucidly described, anthroposophy makes it possible for this empty consciousness to become self-aware, to make sense of itself and thus awaken to a recognition of the other. Sergei Prokofieff was born into the latter part of a century riven with unparalleled cruelty and suffering in order to interpret these same realities to Western humanity in the light of the current world-situation. Thus what Rudolf Steiner brought through anthroposophical spiritual science as a new mystery wisdom and as a means of renewing social and earthly realities was translated by Sergei Prokofieff into an existential path of individual exploration, whereby the idols of materialistic assumptions are consumed in a Christ-centred fire of love. Perhaps all the main themes of Sergei Prokofieff's work—the Christmas Conference of 1923/24 and the Foundation Stone, the mystery of the Resurrection, the Manichaean path of suffering and forgiveness, the mystery of Michael and the rescuing of the cosmic intelligence, the respective tasks of Eastern, Central and Western Europe and their wider significance for human evolution—were brought to a remarkable culmination in his last major work, *The Esoteric Path through the Nineteen Class Lessons*. This is a book which is on the one hand a bold interpretation of the Lessons that Rudolf Steiner gave as the—intended—first part of the esoteric School arising out of the Christmas Conference of 1923/24 and, on the other, a wholly original insight into both the Incarnation of Christ two thousand years ago in Palestine and the so-called supersensible Mystery of Golgotha in the nineteenth century and its aftermath, the possibility for contemporary human beings to perceive Christ in the realm of the etheric. But the core themes for this last book were already present in an earlier book which—perhaps more than any other of his books—was his own individual creation, namely *The Occult Significance of Forgiveness*; and at the heart of this book lies the pain which, as a Russian born into the Soviet era, he had fully explored in his magisterial study of Russian cultural and social history, *The Spiritual Origins of Eastern Europe and the Future Mysteries of the Holy Grail*. I should add that I have been helped in my reflections about my 35 years of active engagement with Sergei Prokofieff's thoughts and writings by the grace of having been asked by Peter Selg to translate his substantial book about Sergei's legacy, *The Mysteries of the Future* (published in English in 2021).

It is, of course, one thing to reflect about books that one has translated and quite another to ask how, or whether, the potential that one has come to discern in them through doing so becomes a wider reality among those who read them. However, this brief assessment of his work and legacy may acquire a richer, deeper colouring if I add a few more, personal reflections.

Sergei was absolutely meticulous in the writing and presentations of his manuscripts (I am especially referring to the time when I was translating his Russian manuscripts as opposed to published books in German), where the copious additions and insertions were carefully inscribed with a highly legible hand. One could not have wished for a more gracious, appreciative and collaborative author. This personal relationship with his translator culminated in a conversation that I had with him on Whitsunday 2014 (8 June) about his book referred to earlier, *The Esoteric Path through the Nineteen Class Lessons*, which—it was clear—I would be translating. I had travelled to Dornach in the hope of meeting with him for the last time on that day, while knowing that my visit to Dornach might not be blessed with the meeting for which I was hoping. However, I was granted not merely a brief encounter but a full half-hour of an intimate meeting and farewell in the course of which Sergei spoke about this book which, he especially emphasized, had been, as it were, bestowed upon him as a miraculous inspiration by the spiritual world.

A second precious strand in our relationship lay in the way that he embraced not only me as his translator but my whole family, my wife and five daughters. This began from our first meetings in Newton Dee Camphill Community, Aberdeen, between 1987 and 1991; and I recall with much fondness Sergei's full engagement with the interests and youthful games of our daughters when he was sharing our explorations of the Aberdeenshire countryside, even extending to the naming of a new kitten when the children couldn't agree. He and Astrid then came on at least two occasions to Hoathly Hill Community, Sussex, attending the inauguration of Pericles Translations and Research in May 1992 and welcoming the arrival of our youngest daughter several years later with endless grace and generosity.

Finally, I wish to highlight the enthusiasm with which he met with first Owen Barfield (1898–1997), that great English anthroposophist and philosopher of language, shortly before Barfield's death, and Edith Biermann (1908–2012), a eurythmist and special needs teacher who had witnessed the burning of the first Goetheanum and was probably the last living person to have done so. He had been keen to be introduced to these two people because they had met Rudolf Steiner (even though Barfield's meeting was an encounter from a distance at one of Steiner's lectures). Sergei also made a particular point of attending the Pericles Theatre Company's production at the Goetheanum of Shakespeare's play *Pericles* in 2008, when he laughed uproariously at the comic, bawdy scenes.

Since Sergei's death, these human connections have been supremely fostered in so many ways by his widow Astrid. And in so far as Sergei's legacy does not reside only in the books but speaks directly to the future, I am confident that these human connections will also develop further as new projects of one kind or another emerge in response to the unfolding situation of humanity and the Earth in our time. Moreover, in the light of the conflict currently raging in Ukraine I am aware of Sergei's very clear statements in his book about Dmitri concerning the duplicitous intentions of Western powers (comprising materialistic 'Americanism' and Jesuit-inspired 'Catholicism') to fragment and undermine the integrity of the entity of 'Eastern Europe', which he identifies as the threefold being of Belarus (thinking), Russia (feeling) and Ukraine (will). I ask myself how, now that since 26 July 2014 he has been in the spiritual world, he views the current tragic situation and in what way can his helping guidance be available to those of us on Earth who wish to receive it.

Roger Pauli

Memories of my Friend Sergei

Right from the first days that I knew Sergei he was clear that his incarnation was to be devoted to raising our awareness of the mission of anthroposophy and Rudolf Steiner. Without Sergei I doubt that I would ever have come to a true personal awareness of the Christmas Conference and the deed of Rudolf Steiner in connecting his destiny with that of the Society.

Sergei never ever wanted to obscure Rudolf Steiner. He wanted to be the window through which one can look and see Rudolf Steiner more closely. *'Not me but him.'* I have never known anyone with such devotion to a life task, such high ideals and standards. I never managed to come near to matching the standards that Sergei set as a member of the School for Spiritual Science and yet somehow he was generous enough to not let that impinge on our friendship. I live with regrets for the times when he invited me to deepen conversations and I lacked the presence of mind to respond. For me one measure of his courage in his tasks in this incarnation was what a lonely journey it was for him, how often he had to hold back and not say what was in his heart.

He once said to me when we were speaking about the first fruits of his work on and with anthroposophy and Rudolf Steiner: 'The forgiveness book [*The Occult Significance of Forgiveness*] arose out of my impulse, it is mine!' 'I am so grateful that he left that one for me.' And the later books such as *And the Earth Becomes a Sun, The Mystery of the Resurrection* and the two great Class books on the School of Spiritual Science show how Sergei's creative work points towards the future, towards the direction in which human beings need to develop and transform the material world through their spiritual work. In these late books the discerning student can see how Sergei allows some of his own spiritual insights to elaborate and develop those of Rudolf Steiner, even though he is careful to not allow his personality to intrude in the work. In one of our conversations during his illness he spoke of his relief at finishing a book only to realize (to be told by the spiritual world) that they had another task for him before the relief of crossing the threshold.

The second book on the School of Spiritual Science is the spiritual task that Sergei was given; and he managed to fulfil it regardless of his illness. In our last conversation he said: 'I can now stand before Rudolf Steiner and stand for everything that I could do. I did my task.'

The whole question of the future of the Earth, of matter becoming spirit and of the Resurrection represents a task not only for initiates to take part in but for each one of us. I see this in my professional work with substances, for example with silica in the process of glass-making. Through Sergei I have learnt very, very much that has brought me deepened insights, for which I am very grateful to him.

Why was Sergei born in Russia? He could bring from there a spiritual constitution that is orientated towards the future, towards the spirit, characterized by a melancholic temperament and a capacity for suffering. Moreover, he could experience life under the Soviet regime and gain access to the Christmas Conference of 1923 in Dornach all on his own, fully independently and without prior preparation!

He was deeply connected with the area of the Black Sea and Crimea and continued to be so in the present time extending even from 2014 to the present struggle in Ukraine. His historical and prehistorical studies of Scythianos and Hibernia and of the history of Eastern Europe (Russia) and its spiritual task in the future confirm this.

Rudolf Steiner was a Central European, a person born into this culture. The course of his life and his journeys, especially in Central Europe but also in Northern and Western Europe, indicate this. Where did Sergei travel? In his youth, to the extent that was possible under the conditions of the regime, in Russia from Karelia to Crimea. Then he could journey to England, Switzerland, Germany and later to almost all countries of Europe together with visits to all continents through invitations of anthroposophical groups and Societies. While I had to grow up in England, in order to be able to become familiar with the thinking and essential nature of economic life.

What are the karmic connections of Sergei in this life? He told me that he entered this life with the inner obligation towards Rudolf Steiner, as he himself expressed it. He did as much as it was possible for him to do. It is also true that he enabled me to do as much as I could do in my role as Treasurer for the AS in GB; without Sergei I could not have rebuilt the financial connections of the AS in GB with the GAS. Sergei knew that he had to be incarnated for the culmination of the anthroposophical movement at the end of the twentieth century.

He knew that he wanted to be on Earth when the 'climax' should begin in the anthroposophical movement at the end of the twentieth century. Was Sergei part of this? Yes.

Diana Pauli

Some Notes about Sergei's Contributions to the Class Lessons

Sergei Prokofieff's work has brought many valuable and original insights to anthroposophy, but I would like to focus particularly on the Class Lessons of the School of Spiritual Science.

In the Stourbridge area (UK) we have been working for four years (with a break for Covid) on his second book on the Class, *The Esoteric Path through the Nineteen Class Lessons in the Light of the Supersensible Mystery of Golgotha and the Fifth Gospel*. For each Lesson we give a form of free rendering where Sergei's insights are woven into the Lesson content. This has been inspiring and extremely helpful for our members for two main reasons.

On the simplest level, his explanations have helped us to understand the meaning of the text of the Lesson and mantra, something which is not always straightforward for many people. Very often, we have heard comments such as, 'Oh, so that's what it means!'

But on a deeper level, Sergei has shown us how Christ is present throughout the 19 Lessons, even though His name is only spoken on two or three occasions. The way he quotes sections of the Bible in relation to the Lessons, particularly St John's Gospel, has brought new depth and interest in the School. It is also my belief that Sergei is pointing in this second book to the future of the Class.

I always try silently to picture Sergei in the moment of quiet before the Lesson starts, and I often feel that he is giving a kind of 'oversight' of what takes place. So for our Class members Sergei has given new life and hope for the future.

A more personal memory

On a more personal note, Sergei has been a tremendous help to me with my work with autistic children. I had come to some original ideas about the cause and treatment of autism from a spiritual scientific point of view. However, I did not feel confident, and needed someone with a deep knowledge of anthroposophy to turn to for reassurance.

So I asked Sergei if he would look over my ideas and tell me what he thought. I sent him some notes, and although special education was not really one of his main interests, he went to a great deal of trouble to read the content carefully, and to consider the validity of my ideas. When he replied positively, this became one of the most important factors in encouraging me to continue.

When I have moments of doubt, I often come back in my mind to Sergei, and find renewed strength and courage.

Carina Vaca Zeller

Impressions of a Friendship

Sergei Prokofieff visited us twice in Chile (October 2005 and April 2010). After his intense work of lectures, conversations and spiritual activity we organized a trip each time, so that he could get to know a bit of Chile and regain his strength in a beautiful natural environment. On both occasions Veronica Ortuzar and I accompanied him. From the first trip to the driest desert in the world in the north of Chile: San Pedro de Atacama, I remember that we went to the Valle de la Luna, which is a desert place with beautiful limestone formations, caves and dunes, as well as offering long, beautiful and interesting hiking trails. We went with a guide, who told us that the local people made small piles of flat stones, so that the spirits of the place would be welcoming to them. Sergei immediately made a pile of flat stones. I was very surprised by his plasticity and adaptability to the culture that surrounded him. Something similar happened when on his second trip we organized a meeting with young people in Santiago de Chile; many of them were medical students, others high school students. It was a very heterogeneous group of young people with a more or less intense relationship to anthroposophy. The idea was to have a round-table discussion with questions that the young people had about anthroposophy. I remember that some of the questions were very profound, while others were very mundane (too much so, in my opinion), like questions about sexuality, addictive behaviours, or technology, for example. Some questions, I must admit, made me feel embarrassed, especially because I had to translate them. I would think to myself: how can I translate such a trivial question to someone as profound as Sergei! I was truly amazed at the naturalness and kindness with which he handled every question that was asked of him. He was open and very relaxed, responding in a way that was approachable and far from dogmatic. He showed genuine understanding of the other person's situation and never spoke from a pedestal. Needless to say, the whole experience was a great lesson for me.

During his second visit to Chile (in April 2010), after his intense activities in Santiago, Veronica Ortuzar and I accompanied Sergei to Easter Island so he could explore, recover, and relax for a few days. On the return flight, sitting next to him, the thought suddenly struck me, like a flash of lightning, that it would be important for him to share with the youth—of whom there were many in Santiago connected to anthroposophy—the life of Parsifal and the Grail impulse (which wasn't on the programme). So, I asked him if he could say something about Parsifal and the Grail impulse to a predominantly young audience in Santiago. He said, 'Well, I don't have any notes, but I can say something.' And that's how the lecture on Parsifal and the mystery of the Grail came about, almost spontaneously, without much chance for promotion (it was the next day) and without any preparation. The room was packed, with a predominantly young audience, who were eagerly awaiting the content that Sergei carried in his soul. Without any notes (back then, we didn't use Google for reference, and he also didn't have the habit of going online), he drew from his soul, forming treasure after treasure on Parsifal, and it was almost as if he were speaking about himself. I was translating for him, and I must say, at moments I was awestruck, standing before a being of such purity, so completely united with the story he was telling.

The first time Sergei Prokofieff came to Chile was in October 2005, which is well into spring here. Generally, it rains in winter, and by October, it practically doesn't rain anymore. We had planned a lecture in a rented hall, expecting at least 500 people. It was a public lecture: What Does Anthroposophy Mean for Modern Man? That afternoon, it started to rain in a way I had never seen before in Santiago. It was a thunderstorm, which is also unusual here, and the rain was falling as if buckets of water were being poured from the sky. The water was flowing through the streets, which looked like rivers. I received desperate phone calls from potential attendees saying they couldn't leave their homes to go to the lecture because of the amount of water running through the streets. Clearly, this wasn't normal, and I was extremely worried, as it was the only public lecture, and this was happening right then. I thought, no one is going to come. I don't know how, but at least 250 people showed up. Without the rain, we surely would have exceeded 600. Sergei gave a wonderful lecture, right in the midst of the rain. The next day, his flight was leaving in the afternoon. My plan was to take him by car to a small hill (San Cristóbal) in the middle of the city to show him Santiago from above. I took him, though I wasn't too hopeful about seeing much, as it was still somewhat cloudy. When we got to the top, the sky cleared in an incredible way, and the Andes Mountains appeared in all their magnificence, dressed in pure radiant white, beautifully framing the city of Santiago, which was glowing in unusual colours through crystal-clear air. It was as if the city had dressed itself up to bid farewell to Sergei Prokofieff in a festival of nature, thanking him for all the spiritual work he had gifted us. He was very happy with this beautiful farewell that the city of Santiago in consort with nature had taken great care to give him.

Sergei had a wonderful way of combining a very deep and serious side, almost stern, with another very human side, light, and full of humour. These little stories I'm about to share are from when we were in San Pedro de Atacama. We were about to go to the Geysers, and before we went, I wanted to explain to Sergei what they were about. My German isn't great—good enough to get by but not fluent enough to say everything I want with ease. At the same time, I had heard some news about some foreigners who had fallen into boiling water and died. So I explained to Sergei that when we went to the Geysers, he shouldn't get too close to the edge of the hot springs because there had been some foreigners who did that, fell in, and were 'cooked' (I couldn't find a better word to express it in German). He then replied, full of humour: 'Yes, can you imagine? You'd have to send a cooked Prokofieff back to the Vorstand.' (At that time, he was still part of the Vorstand.)

The other story, which I found really amusing, was when we were driving in a van along some high-altitude roads with a guide. Sergei kept asking, 'How high are we here?' He wanted to know when we had reached the highest point. Then, at one point, the guide said: 'This is the highest point.' I think it was around 4,200 metres above sea level (or 4,700?). So I said to Sergei, 'Come on, let's get out, and now we're going to run.' I started running across the plain at that altitude, and to my great surprise, Sergei ran with me. These are unforgettable experiences because you get to know the depth of his thought and soul, but at the same time, he was willing to take part in these everyday moments, sprinkled with humour.

When we were on Easter Island, one of our first outings was to a beach called Anakena. It's a small beach with white sand, palm trees, moais in the background (the iconic stone statues of Easter Island), and a sea with warm, transparent water. In short, it's a paradise-like landscape. Sergei told me that he loved the sea and that he enjoyed swimming in the ocean. I went into the water a bit, like people typically do, where the waves are. Sergei began swimming toward the deeper part of the sea, and out there, where there were no more waves and the water was deep, he started swimming back and forth. He spent a long time swimming. I was very surprised by this, because even though I don't consider myself fearful, going that far out into the sea struck me as an act of unusual courage. The next day, we went on another outing in the morning, returning by early afternoon. But Sergei wanted to go back to Anakena beach at the end of the day. It brought him such joy; he was almost like a child when we told him we'd go back to Anakena at the end of the day. The same thing happened the next day, and every day we were on Easter Island; he wanted to go to the deep sea at the end of whatever was planned for the day. I admit, I only joined him once. That feeling of infinity and unfathomable depth made me a bit uneasy. Perhaps that's what attracted him so much. Later, I reflected that this sensation might be similar to what Rudolf Steiner describes as spiritual experiences.

Here in Chile, before Sergei came, there was historically an extremely marked polarization within the anthroposophical movement. When he came to Chile for the first time, the first thing he wanted to do was visit, greet, and converse as a friend with the key figures from the different groups here, recognizing each one for their work. There were two main groups, which found it totally impossible to connect with one another. When Sergei Prokofieff's visit was announced and open lectures were organized for anyone who wanted to come, in a large public venue, people from both groups showed up, and for the first time in the history of anthroposophy in Chile, there were individuals from both polarized groups under the same roof. While this didn't mean cordial relationships were established there, I already felt it was a blessing just to be sitting in the same audience, under the same roof, listening to a lecture of spiritual content. A spirituality as profound as Sergei's created the space for this first encounter to happen. It was like melting an ice that seemed almost impossible to thaw.

After that, other activities involving joint participation began to take shape, and this has happened more and more frequently. That drastic division between groups no longer exists—although there are still different groups working in diverse ways, there are increasingly more human-to-human connections between them. At the same time, more groups have formed. The new generations today can't even imagine how drastic the division was in the past or the profound significance of that first moment, under one roof, under one spirituality. I truly believe that only a soul radiating as much spiritual warmth as Sergei Prokofieff's could have achieved something like that.

Sergei was one of those people who could say a single phrase, and it would leave a deep imprint on your heart. I remember that during one of his trips to Chile, we held a gathering for conversation among anthroposophists and him. It was a large circle, and people asked him all kinds of questions. One woman, who had been involved with anthroposophy for many years, asked: 'Mr. Prokofieff, now with all the cell phones and artificial radiation, don't you think this interferes and makes meditation—that is, our connection to the spiritual world—much more difficult?' Sergei responded with something that has stayed with me forever. He said: 'Without a doubt, all the radiation makes meditation harder, but the I is stronger.' I should mention that I am very involved in activism to protect people's health from radiation and to ensure that technology develops responsibly. But within me, Sergei's thought—'but the I is stronger'—encourages me to always keep in mind that all my external activism in this matter must be balanced by an inner practice that makes my I stronger, and that inspires the I in many others to also strive to be stronger.

Another time, when Sergei was already very ill and he knew that his passage through the threshold was likely not far off, I visited him, and we had a beautiful conversation. We began talking about death, and he said to me: 'You know, I know so much about death thanks to everything Rudolf Steiner has revealed to us, that I go toward that path full of anticipation.' Sergei said this to me as if he had planned the most interesting journey in the world, and he was eager for all he would experience and see there. This conversation also left a deep mark on my heart, and it shines like a beacon of light every time I reflect on the topic of death.

Rebecca McGrath

Impressions of Sergei Prokofieff

When a member of the Anthroposophical Society in America heard that this book would appear in English translation, Rebecca McGrath sent me some of her impressions of Sergei Prokofieff which she had gathered from her experiences as a student at the Goetheanum and from participating in events with him in America. The following represents excerpts from her lengthy letter which I have edited. I think that many other members and friends would support her impressions wholeheartedly.

Virginia Sease

In Sacramento when he was lecturing about his book *May Human Beings Hear It!* I could observe him from a distance and could sense his quiet humility. Never drawing attention to himself he seemed almost embarrassed when the USA anthroposophists wanted him to sign his books. Of course, he did so courteously but with a certain hesitation in a humble way as I witnessed. When we were at lunch it was very hot, but he still kept his blazer on when everyone else was loose and comfortable, that is, he respected the reason why he was there. He maintained a certain idealism in his appearance.

Sergei Prokofieff's gentle kindness was evident in the way he moved in situations—never disrupting but always within the flow with quiet observation of everything happening around him. I found this refreshing to witness. When he spoke it was objective, never about himself nor out of sentimentality. The content which he brought was set free to be awakened by the listener. It seemed as if he spoke from a higher plane, and we had to reach up with our thinking to be within it in freedom. He never 'talked down' to his audience and I experienced his words as filled with life—be it in a lecture or in his writings. His conscious but selfless approach could allow Rudolf Steiner's words to stream into the world—words of Christ and Michael as they could live through a human being.

A complete harmony can be seen from his first books to his last in which anthroposophy can be deepened for the individual reader. Often this could occur through his working with a dichotomy of questions to find the harmony between the polarities and providing the answer out of anthroposophy through true spiritual thinking. This was the case for Sergei Prokofieff's research: it weaves seamlessly together with what Rudolf Steiner had given to us. In all of his works Sergei Prokofieff constantly reminds us that the path is through anthroposophy by means of thinking into the sphere of Michael-Christ. In order to respect his rare moments of privacy I only spoke directly to him three times: I can remember them vividly like yesterday. I can even hear his voice within me to this day.

I am grateful that I was able to perceive Sergei Prokofieff in the USA and at the Goetheanum. I saw how everyone would pull on him and I never wanted to be among them, so I held back from interactions so that he could have his own space. It was a blessing to attend his funeral, and I felt a deep karmic connection with him. This is the case for many people whose destiny allowed them to access the works of Sergei Prokofieff and/or to experience him personally. I read his books like I do Rudolf Steiner's, over and over again. He leads us to the places where we can discover many aspects of cosmic wisdom in Rudolf Steiner's work because he shared his research, such as in the footnotes, with us; thereby we can become little by little independent researchers ourselves.

Finally, I would like to express my gratitude to Sergei Prokofieff as an example of how it is possible through true devotion, humility and unceasing work to fathom ever more fully the gift of Rudolf Steiner's anthroposophy.

Rebecca McGrath, Nevada, USA, December 2024

Ulrich Oelssner

Building with Sergei Prokofieff

After the renovations of the hall of the Goetheanum in 2002, Sergei Prokofieff asked me whether I could imagine building a house for him here in Dornach. The difficulty of his was that he had had a library specially adapted to his needs built in his existing house which would have to be wholly incorporated in the new house. This made me curious. Without further ado I decided to go to where he lived in Bad Boll in order to view the existing situation for myself and to receive an impression of his living space.

He later admitted to me that this visit was decisive in leading him to think that I was the right one to design the house for him in Dornach. With this began a time of many discussions and meetings, from which I came to know him to be a sensitive, refined and highly cultured person. It was therefore highly exciting for me to gain through this building project a totally different insight into the 'Russian soul', in that this was by no means a wooden house (for a wooden house is a dacha); the hall was to be the centre from where the rooms open out, the library would be a realm in its own right, the bench around the stove would have its essential place in the kitchen. This reminded me of the descriptions of my grandparents and of my father, who was born and grew up in Moscow.

Sergei Prokofieff placed much importance on the shaping of the details, for example the front doors, the wall of bookshelves, the watercourse in the garden or the external lighting. Everything was pursued with great attention and to some extent in partnership.

In the course of subsequent, mostly unplanned encounters during walks, in the field or in woodland, I was always again touched by how trustingly he opened himself up to me at a time of great difficulties and disputes. All these encounters form part of my unforgettable memories of Sergei Prokofieff.

Christiane and Martin Wigand

Sergei Prokofieff in South Africa

It was in the year 1998, thus over 20 years ago. Much has meanwhile been forgotten, but some experiences with Sergei Prokofieff continue to be a living memory for us. Martin was at the time responsible for the Rudolf Steiner Centre in Johannesburg, where Sergei gave an evening lecture for members of the Society. He entered the well-attended space, went up to the lectern, directed his eyes to a point in the distance above the heads of the listeners and began his lecture in English. We no longer recall the content, only that he spoke in a polished manner: every word, every sentence was precisely formulated, even though he never looked at his notes but always directed his attention to the same distant point. Moreover, he did not exceed his allotted time by so much as a minute. Yes, we thought this was a very well-prepared lecture, delivered with perfect concentration. Afterwards he wanted to be taken immediately to where he was staying. What the lecturer concealed was that he was struggling with an attack of migraine.

We wanted to show Sergei and his wife Astrid something of South Africa, and so the four of us journeyed for some days to the famous Kruger Park, which is half the size of Switzerland and is a place where African animals go about freely while people have to remain in their cars. Sergei and Astrid slept in an African roundhouse with a bath and kitchen, while we spent the night in a tent. In the morning we got up early and prepared breakfast together with Astrid, while Sergei was still meditating. Then we went for a 'game drive'. While the three of us were observing lions and other animals, Sergei had his English-Russian dictionary on his lap and was enlarging his English vocabulary. Only when we enthusiastically shouted 'lion' or 'elephant' did he look briefly out of the window.

On the journey home Martin asked him a question about Rudolf Steiner's relationship to other great initiates. His answer made a great impression on us: an hour's lecture in German, wholly impromptu! We then experienced how strongly he lived with these themes and was ready to speak about them at any time. This was our impression: a person who had wholly internalized anthroposophy to the point where he could speak extensively, directly and spontaneously out of its rich abundance.

Thomas O'Keefe

In Memory of My Life-Encounter with Sergei O. Prokofieff

I encountered Sergei Prokofieff's work in 2006 as a college student, shortly after discovering anthroposophy. The first book by him that I read was *The Encounter with Evil and Its Overcoming through Spiritual Science*. During this time, I was particularly driven to seek an understanding of the meaning of evil in world evolution, and this book was deeply helpful to me in that pursuit. Upon studying his work, I could sense in Sergei Prokofieff's way of writing that he is someone who lives anthroposophy with deep earnestness and represents it in the world with the dedication of his whole being.

I was so struck by the calibre of this quality in his writing that I decided to read all of his other books over the course of the next few years. This was naturally a great challenge, though the enthusiasm I experienced during this study continually propelled me forward. I gained immeasurably much from reading *Rudolf Steiner and the Founding of the New Mysteries, Eternal Individuality: Towards a Karmic Biography of Novalis, The Cycle of the Year as a Path of Initiation, The Heavenly Sophia and the Being Anthroposophia, The Occult Significance of Forgiveness, May Human Beings Hear It!*, and especially *The Spiritual Origins of Eastern Europe and the Future Mysteries of the Holy Grail.*

His work felt to me like an intensified tour of the most essential themes within anthroposophy. The depth and expansive scope with which he wove his thoughts about these themes together with related quotations from Rudolf Steiner's life-work enabled a profound overview of the living tapestry of Rudolf Steiner's spiritual-scientific knowledge.

I experienced that Sergei Prokofieff was able to 'lift' his capacity of thinking into the realm of spiritual-scientific thoughts in such a way that he could freely and livingly engage his thinking within this realm in a way that followed a certain cosmic order. It is a 'spiritualized thinking' that also incorporates feeling and will. This led to his unique ability to develop a comprehensive context through which to understand the often fragmentary pictures that Rudolf Steiner paints throughout his various books and lecture cycles. Rudolf Steiner occasionally mentioned this type of synthesizing activity as being helpful to the development of anthroposophy: 'It is possible to expand what has been briefly outlined here by means of the numerous details that you will find in my lecture cycles and writings. Not much has yet been done to that effect ....'[17] This capacity also led to Sergei Prokofieff's ability to occasionally work his way toward new spiritual-scientific insights by bringing together and 'thinking further' various insights found throughout Rudolf Steiner's work. This active, spiritualized study activity was once succinctly characterized by Rudolf Steiner as 'to some extent engaging in spiritual research'.[18]

Ernst Lehrs reports:

> Rudolf Steiner was once asked by a friend how one could know that one had begun to engage in spiritual research. He replied by asking the person in question whether the following [situation] had happened to him: whether in his work with anthroposophy he had encountered

---

[17]GA 316, January 5, 1924.

[18]See the full quotation below.

> a truth that struck him and remained livingly in his memory, then after some time another truth had similarly impressed him, and out of the coming together of the two, an insight had occurred to him which derived from the substance of both. This, acknowledged the questioner, had been one of the most satisfying and assuring events of his anthroposophical studies. In such a moment, Rudolf Steiner explained to him, he had been to some extent engaging in spiritual research.[19]

What impressed me most about Sergei Prokofieff's attitude in his written work was his uncompromising willingness to address the qualities and nuances of the various forces of evil. He did this in a selfless and courageous way, forthrightly addressing not only the spiritual existence of counter-forces in the form of Lucifer, Ahriman, and so forth, but also the topic of the diverse streams of occult brotherhoods and their influence on the course of human evolution. He did this whenever the topic he was writing about called for such awareness—which it often did—and he did so on the basis of a careful reference to Rudolf Steiner's many deep and nuanced characterizations. His courage in addressing these themes likely arose in part from his deep feeling for the Christ event of our time. Like Rudolf Steiner, Sergei Prokofieff considered the Christ event of the twentieth century to be deeply connected with the archetypal human challenge of encountering the mystery of evil—that is, the challenge of becoming mature and courageous enough to grapple with this mystery inwardly in conscious thought. Judging by the attitude evident in Sergei Prokofieff's work, my sense is that the grave encounter with evil, and the accompanying deep feeling for the supersensible Christ event of our time that can emerge through this encounter, belonged to the most central themes of his life.[20]

In 2008, a friend and I visited Dornach for the first time. I managed to attend a study group led by Sergei Prokofieff in the Goetheanum,

---

[19]Ernst Lehrs, *Gelebte Erwartung* ['Lived Anticipation'] (Mellinger, 1979), p. 320. Quoted in Sergei O. Prokofieff, *The Mystery of John the Baptist and John the Evangelist at the Turning Point of Time* (Temple Lodge, 2005), p. 11f.

[20]For Rudolf Steiner's insight into the relation between powerlessness in the encounter with evil and the Christ event of our time, see the end of the lecture of 16 October 1918 entitled 'How Do I Find the Christ?', in: Rudolf Steiner, *Death as Metamorphosis of Life* (SteinerBooks, 2008), GA 182.

and afterward I waited to ask him if he would be willing to meet with me for conversation. He suggested that I contact his secretary, but when I told him I would only be in Dornach for the next week or so, he invited me up to his office and took out his calendar, and we agreed on a time. On the day of our meeting, we discussed some of the themes within his writings—especially the mystery of the Foundation Stone Meditation, which he entered into with great enthusiasm. I was particularly struck by what he said about the depth and expansiveness of this mystery. He said something to the effect of the following: As I increasingly immerse myself in the mystery of the Foundation Stone Meditation year after year, I discover more and more depth to this mystery, to the point that I have found it to be an inexhaustible source of wisdom. Every time I meditatively live with a question related to it and receive something in the direction of an answer, there soon follow more questions, then more indications toward an answer, and so forth. And I come to realize again and again that this mystery is deeper and greater still than I had ever imagined.[21]

But more memorable than the conversation itself was something that Sergei Prokofieff wanted to show to my friend and me. He invited us to come back a few days later to meet him again, whereupon he led us into the room where Rudolf Steiner crossed the threshold of death, known as the atelier. In the solemn and spiritually full atmosphere of that room, there stood a vase of red roses in front of a small stand made of wood, upon which was placed the death-mask of Rudolf Steiner. Nearby, there was a smaller stand on which was placed a hand-carved wooden picture frame in the shape of a pentagon. The frame had a small double-framed door that could be opened and closed over the picture. Sergei Prokofieff opened it for us, revealing a picture of Rudolf Steiner on his death bed shortly after crossing the threshold. As he opened the picture frame and stepped back to let us look at it more closely, a deep sorrow came over us all. He was visibly moved by this experience of encountering the event of Rudolf Steiner's death—an experience that he must have had many times before. I was moved as well—both by this encounter with the event of Rudolf Steiner's death, and by the way Sergei Prokofieff experienced this.

---

[21]This is not a direct quote, but my recollection of the essence of what was said, to the best of my knowledge.

Looking back on that meeting, it becomes increasingly clear to me why Sergei Prokofieff wanted to give us a chance to experience this room and the remaining earthly artefacts related to Rudolf Steiner's death. He wanted to let us have an experience of the quality of that tragic event—that event and mystery which can move one deeply and can vividly colour one's inner attitude toward anthroposophy and Rudolf Steiner. To experience this room with him was far more powerful, far more revealing of the underlying impulse motivating his life's work, than any conversation could be. If there is one moment that, to me, encapsulates the being of Sergei O. Prokofieff—and which perfectly reflects the quality of earnestness and devotion that I experienced in his books—it is this. Those books could only have been written by someone who felt this degree of pain born of love upon encountering the event of Rudolf Steiner's death. And, although I could not put it into words at the time, that is why his written work had immediately struck me as something so rare and valuable. Reading his books is far more than an intellectual experience—it is also an experience of this quality of love and devotion to Rudolf Steiner, to anthroposophy, to the spiritual beings standing behind them, and to the unfinished tasks that still connect Rudolf Steiner, from across the threshold, with all those who share his life-aims. In Sergei Prokofieff's books, all three powers of the soul are called upon and stirred to a high degree—thinking, feeling, and willing—and the powers of the will can receive an especially strengthening and awakening impulse in this experience.

The way Sergei Prokofieff experienced Rudolf Steiner's death is not only a matter of the sorrow and pain that one can experience upon losing a beloved friend and teacher. Bound up with it is also a deep feeling for the sacrifices that Rudolf Steiner made in his final attempt to give an enduring spiritual impulse to humanity through the re-founding of the Anthroposophical Society at the Christmas Conference of 1923/24, as well as a feeling for the many attacks and hindrances that he had to bear both from outside the Society and from members within it—the latter including both a lack of wakeful understanding as well as an unconscious 'inner opposition' to what Rudolf Steiner was trying to achieve. All of this culminated in the tragedy of Rudolf Steiner's early departure from the earth, a theme which Sergei Prokofieff understood on a profound level and had written about extensively in all its aspects.[22] I felt that his sorrow at the event of Rudolf Steiner's death embodied a feeling of the overarching tragedy that we—Rudolf Steiner's friends, colleagues, and students—lacked the necessary inner strength and inner activity to offer him protection through our spiritually deepened understanding of what he was trying to achieve, the various forces that stood against him, what he was risking as a result of his sacrifices, and the nature of the support that he stood in need of.[23]

During this first visit to Dornach, I also had a chance to see Sergei Prokofieff give a speech at the annual *Totenfeier* (a celebration and remembrance of the lives of those who have died). It was in German, which at that time I could barely understand. This is the one and only lecture that I was ever able to witness by Sergei Prokofieff. What struck me most about it was the warmth, devotion, and intensity in his tone of voice, as well as the way he gripped the podium as he spoke. I had the impression that he gripped the podium in order to ground himself physically on the earth while in spirit he was active in experiencing and delivering what he had to say. It gave me a strong impression of what a powerful and deeply human activity it can be to convey one's own thoughts through the spoken word.

When I visited Dornach again for the second time, in spring of 2011, I had planned on attending his course for the students of the English Studies programme on the theme of the Christmas Conference and the Foundation Stone Meditation. It was with great sadness that I learned, upon arriving, that he had become too ill to teach the course.

During the Holy Nights of 2011/2012, I undertook a study of Sergei Prokofieff's book *The Mystery of the Resurrection in the Light of Anthroposophy*. Filled with enthusiasm, I resolved to write a comprehensive review of it. My review ended up being a 12-page elaboration of what I felt to be the most important elements of this impressive work. I sent my review to him to ask for his thoughts. His written reply contained a lesson that stays strongly with me to this day. He appreciated what

---

[22]See especially his books *Rudolf Steiner and the Founding of the New Mysteries* and *May Human Beings Hear It!*, as well as Supplement V in the latter book.
[23]In his book *Rudolf Steiner and the Founding of the New Mysteries*, Sergei Prokofieff draws a powerful analogy here in relation to the way Christ's disciples could not remain awake through the final stages of His sacrifice.

I had written; however, he emphasized that 'a review has not the primary task to communicate the content of the book, but much more to reveal the thoughts and the feelings which the reviewer experienced during the reading of the book.... Therefore, a review becomes a creative deed.'[24]

In 2012, while I was a student at The Christian Community Seminary in Spring Valley, NY, I came across a German-language summary of a lecture that Sergei Prokofieff, still recovering from his illness, had given at the commemoration of Rudolf Steiner's Death Day on 30 March of that year in the Great Hall of the Goetheanum. I had begun to learn German in the years prior, and I was very interested to know what Sergei Prokofieff had to say, so I undertook a translation with the help of a friend. His lecture focussed on the importance of standing up for Rudolf Steiner against public defamation, and described the way in which the lack of heartfelt care and wakeful defence in response to such attacks was a source of great pain for Rudolf Steiner in the years leading up to his death. (The defamation of Rudolf Steiner was especially prevalent in 2011 as a result of the events surrounding his 150th birthday commemoration and the public attention this drew to the Goetheanum.[25]) The implication was clear: the members of the Society are currently confronted in a similar way with the inner question: 'How do we stand before Rudolf Steiner today?'[26]—How do we feel, spiritually, when we perceive that untruths and distortions are publicly proclaimed about him? Does this cause us pain or do we remain indifferent?—His lecture also raised the serious question of the extent to which we are able and willing to give an authentic answer to this question—an answer that comes from a spiritually real inner connection. In order to achieve such an inner connection out of which an authentic answer could emerge, old habits of thought and soul would have to be recognized and overcome, among them: the over-eagerness to

[24]From a personal letter of 9 March, 2012.

[25]See *Crisis in the Anthroposophical Society and Pathways to the Future* (Temple Lodge, 2013), Part I: 'The Identity of the General Anthroposophical Society' by Peter Selg.

[26]See ibid., Part II: 'How Do We Stand before Rudolf Steiner Today?' by Sergei O. Prokofieff.

appear 'non-dogmatic' in the eyes of Rudolf Steiner's critics today; the resentment towards the reverent attitude often shown to Rudolf Steiner by serious students of his work; and, at times, even a hidden, often unconscious desire to see Rudolf Steiner torn down from an imagined pedestal.

Peter Selg had joined Sergei Prokofieff in giving a lecture in which he offered similarly direct words on this theme. At that moment in the history of the Society, these two were for the most part seen from official quarters as troublemakers—or worse, as psychologically unhinged—for their very clear statements. To my view, they were attempting to awaken the conscience of the active members of the Society in a way that distinguished them as individualities of especially high spiritual integrity, as they clearly placed their striving for truth and their love of Rudolf Steiner above the inevitable social consequences and defamation of their own character. Their statements went against the grain of public opinion, which at that time was hardly distinguishable from the prevailing attitude with which the work and aims of the Anthroposophical Society were directed.

This clear and selfless love of truth that transcends the fears and concerns of the personality, and that is prepared to take principled action following from one's sense of truth and justice—this is a striking and characteristic attribute of Sergei Prokofieff. He seemed to experience a love of truth—and a pain at untruthfulness—to a special degree of intensity. His attitude in this regard reminds me of what I feel to be one of Rudolf Steiner's most essential spiritual-scientific descriptions—found in Chapter 3 of the book *The Stages of Higher Knowledge*. Here Rudolf Steiner describes in detail the importance of cultivating a deep and personal love of truth, and an aversion toward untruth, as a prerequisite for developing the capacity of inspiration.

> Quite systematically must the esoteric student turn his attention to his soul life, and he must bring it to the point where logical error is a source of *pain* to him that in no way falls short of physical pain; and conversely, the 'right' must bring him real joy or delight. Thus, where another only brings his intellect, his power of judgement, into movement, the esoteric student must learn to live through the whole sequence of feelings, from pain to enthusiasm, from the excruciating tension to the delightful resolution in the possession of truth. Indeed, he must learn to feel something like hatred toward what the 'nor-

> mal' person experiences only in a cold and sober way as 'incorrect'; he must develop within himself a *love* of truth that bears an entirely personal character; as personal, as warm, as the lover feels for the beloved.[27]

Right to the end, Sergei Prokofieff was deeply affected by the lack of understanding and support he received from the leading circles of the Anthroposophical Society when he increasingly emphasized the importance of a spiritually real relationship with Rudolf Steiner—not least when it came to taking an active stance in the face of public defamation of Rudolf Steiner. The fact that he felt such a lack of understanding and support would become increasingly clear to me years later in conversation with him. Looking at his situation from the outside, I would never have imagined how profoundly lonely he felt in his apparently powerful position on the Executive Council of the Goetheanum, especially in his final years.

Since I did not see a clear path to having my translated reports about Sergei Prokofieff and Peter Selg's lectures printed in the English-language anthroposophical newsletters that I knew of, and since I felt time was of the essence, I created a new newsletter, called *Deepening Anthroposophy*, in order to quickly make them available to the English-speaking members of the Anthroposophical Society. At that time, I was not fully aware of the etiquette for such endeavours, and whether permission was needed to start a newsletter for members. I wrote a letter to Sergei Prokofieff to ask for his view on my idea, and he warmly gave his full support to it, saying that no permission is needed, and that it is a matter of individual freedom for members to start their own initiatives.

I was able to visit Dornach again for an extended period over the following two years, during which I was able to meet with Sergei Prokofieff for conversation several times, up until soon before he crossed the threshold of death on 26 July, 2014. From these conversations, the moment that lives most strongly in my memory is when I asked him how he goes about preparing his lectures. He stood up, invited me to follow him to his work desk in his library, and pulled out a small piece of paper on which was drawn a fairly elaborate symbolic pic-

---

[27]Rudolf Steiner, *The Stages of Higher Knowledge* (GA 12), Ch. 3: 'Inspiration'. This translation revised by TO.

ture. He told me that he prepares his lectures in three steps. First, he researches and writes an extensive outline of everything he wants to address. Then, he reduces this outline to a smaller list of key points, each encapsulating an essential theme within the whole. Finally, he further transforms this list of key points into a symbolic picture which encompasses the whole of the lecture. This picture is what he brings with him to the podium, as the 'key' from which he is able to derive the whole content of his preparatory work and research.

In all his many aspects and attributes—especially in his love of truth and his depth of devotion—Sergei O. Prokofieff appeared to me as a most earnestly striving representative of anthroposophy. I also felt him to be like an archetypal student of anthroposophy and Rudolf Steiner. I feel that a core aspect of his mission was to demonstrate to all future students of anthroposophy what Rudolf Steiner emphasized many times throughout his writings: that clairvoyance is not required to understand the results of spiritual-scientific research, that one's own sense of truth can develop into a powerful organ of perception when working with the content of spiritual science, and that this continual inner activity gives rise to a new, living understanding of the world that leads to ever new and deeper insights.[28] Through his work, Sergei Prokofieff has shown how intelligence is able to spiritualize itself—how working with the substance of spiritual-scientific research can develop a living, generative way of thinking. Anyone who deeply and earnestly takes up a study of anthroposophy knows that this is fundamentally possible, that the experience of reading and *striving to comprehend* awakens deeper and more subtle powers of the soul and especially of the thinking capacity. One of the most striking instances where Rudolf Steiner emphasized this reality is in his 1925 Preface to *An Outline of Occult Science*:

> I have quite consciously endeavoured not to offer a 'popular' exposition, but rather an exposition that makes it necessary for the reader to study the content with strict effort of thought. The character I impressed upon my books is such that their very study is the begin-

---

[28]This latent capacity of knowledge that can emerge from the human soul forces in the course of living into the results of spiritual-scientific research is perhaps best characterized in the fourth chapter of Rudolf Steiner's book *Theosophy*, entitled 'The Path of Knowledge'.

> ning of spiritual training. For the calm, conscious effort of thought that this reading makes necessary strengthens the forces of the soul and through this makes them capable of approaching the spiritual world.[29]

Sergei Prokofieff demonstrated to us the breathtaking extent to which this capacity of spiritualized thinking can be developed when cultivated with enthusiasm, dedication, and devotion.

Ursula Heusser

Sergei Prokofieff and Eurythmy

Through Sergei Prokofieff's books and especially through his personal presence as a member of the Vorstand at the Goetheanum, the impulse of the Christmas Conference and the Foundation Stone has been brought to many countries. This has enabled a worldwide impulse to engage actively with the laying of the Foundation Stone to arise. Sergei also worked at that time together with us eurythmists at the Goetheanum. Through his great Christian and cosmological background and knowledge he was able to solve many mysteries in Rudolf Steiner's indications, such as in the indications for the eurythmy forms, sounds and colours in relation to the words of the Foundation Stone Meditation. He therefore made it possible for us to understand the indications of the Goetheanum stage, which have been strictly handed down, in a new way and, hence, to implement them with a renewed, personal enthusiasm. We felt inwardly strengthened and carried by Sergei's explanations at a time when our classical, tradition-laden eurythmy was made an object of ridicule by many. Through his explanations I again received the courage to seek the acknowledgement for my path in eurythmy and for my way of struggling with visible speech and visible singing within myself, in recognition of the unique nature of the eurythmy impulse and in striving towards the source out of which it was created.

---

[29]GA 13, Tr. H. Monges (Anthroposophic Press, 1972), p. xiii.

BONS MOTS AND ANECDOTES

Charlotte Blume

Thoughts grow together

I don't have any written testimonies of Sergei Prokofieff, but I carry much of him within my soul. From his writings I experienced for the first time that thoughts can grow together. If one engages with a thought and enters into it with one's whole soul, one also arrives at a goal, a deeper encounter, and before one loses sight of it one grows into a further series of thoughts. In all clarity it is like the symbiosis of plants, the respective thoughts have a living connection with one another. The second thing that I often experienced when I was able to hear him was that in his presence I could experience a thought more deeply in a moral sense than I was able to purely out of my own personal orientation.

Konstanze Volbehr

Displeased

One memory that I have of Sergei Prokofieff is of an Easter Sunday many years ago, when he was giving the morning lecture during an Easter conference at the Goetheanum. It was the first and last time that I experienced Sergei Prokofieff being displeased with something.

Why? This particular year the clocks went forward precisely during the night before Easter, and this was the reason why he wholly humanly gave vent to his feelings before he went on to speak to us in his familiar positive, loving, profound and true manner.

Robert Veitenthal

Competence and Intellectual Assurance

Robert Veitenthal added the following note at the end of a detailed report from November 1986:

Youthful, thin gracefully Nordic appearance. The somewhat broken German with a Russian accent does not detract from the clarity and profundity of the train of thoughts. The lecturer speaks very seriously, impressively, convincingly and powerfully from an extensive knowledge of Rudolf Steiner's work. It is not only referred to and quoted from. Behind what he says one can discern an independent experience and an intimate connection with the objective essence of anthroposophy. It is spoken out of a basic competence and intellectual assurance, mostly completely freely.

One has the particular impression of being addressed by a true representative of the Slavic Russian Folk-soul, which has the task of developing the Spirit-self in the sixth post-Atlantean period.

After the lecture there was no loud applause, as is often the general custom. The deeply impressed and inspired listeners persisted for a long time in a thoughtful, impassioned silence, pervaded with a festive, consecrated mood. Several participants had the need personally to express their gratitude to the speaker.

Stefania Bergamini

When abroad

Stefania Bergamini makes the following observation in her reminiscences of Sergei Prokofieff in Milan:

What struck me increasingly was that when abroad he became a different person—in my eyes he was more relaxed, more open and somehow freer; in Dornach I experienced him to be tenser in his behaviour and in his voice, and it was as though he had put on iron armour and a helmet.

Helga Fehling

Presence of mind in everyday circumstances

I gladly write of a little incident which—amidst much that was more significant—came spontaneously to mind when I heard the news of Sergei Prokofieff's death.

It was during a performance in the Great Hall, when suddenly a cry of panic suddenly rang out from the gallery: 'There's a fire!' Could flames be seen up amidst the lights? I'm not sure. Before anyone could turn round, Sergei Prokofieff jumped up from the front row and rushed with giant strides up the steps at the side. Very quickly the defect was remedied and the performance was able to continue undisturbed.

Hans Hasler

Together

My first sight of Sergei was during those lectures that he gave in the student house during his first comet-like appearance in Dornach shortly after Christmas 1981. I did not appreciate the somewhat sentimental way that his protector Annie Jahn lit a candle in the middle of the packed, somewhat darkened hall; but the lecture and above all the way that Sergei spoke I found quite riveting.

Some years later we stayed together in Ruth and Georg Unger's guest house several times during conferences. We had some deep conversations about Russian translations of Rudolf Steiner's meditations. Sergei loved the German language and regarded it as the most suitable language for esoteric substance in our time. For my part I loved the Russian language. And so there was a stimulus for mutual understanding. But this enthusiasm also extended to purely mundane matters. Sergei wanted to know how I managed to knot my tie so precisely and symmetrically. There were also some shortcomings in the impressive way that he dressed; and I showed him what these were.

We subsequently met—other than in Dornach, of course—in various places in Eastern Europe at conferences that we attended together and where we both gave lectures: Tbilisi in Georgia, Sofia in Bulgaria, Riga in Latvia. I particularly recall the conversations about the laborious coming into being of the Society in Georgia. The debates went on for days in wearisomely long meetings; our departure was fixed and we already doubted whether the founding would happen at all. We therefore decided to undertake a wonderful excursion to Kasbegi the day before our departure; and it was on this very day that the preparations took a decisive step further. The by no means smooth process of the founding then occurred when we were already in the aeroplane the following day.

Although Sergei had an excellent understanding of the German language, it always continued to be a foreign language for him. Many friends were disturbed by a certain inflexibility of intonation in the lectures that he gave in German, and the often almost jolting effect was experienced as aggravating for many ears. It was therefore a special experience to hear him lecture in Russian. The flow of the speech was far more relaxed, natural and less laborious; one could then experience a use of words that was to a high degree artistically formed.

Manfred Heid

A good piece of advice: humour

Following the end of a long letter about Sergei Prokofieff's lectures:

Since I am in the flow of writing, I should like to conclude by adding something that I should like to say to you alone.

Do not take this as petty criticism but, rather, as the loving advice of a good friend. It concerns the following matter. It has struck me that when you are driving towards the climax in your lectures, some people go to sleep. This is not the case with me; I can listen to you for hours. Both in your written and verbal presentations, I always admire that you have the great ability—unmatched by hardly anyone else—to embrace vast perspectives over a wide area, thus extending a giant arc as Bruckner does in his symphonies. You are a 'Bruckner of the word'. But not all—perhaps only few—people are able to follow you.

What advice does Rudolf Steiner give to a teacher? That one unremittingly feeds the pupil with powerful, serious substance, but inserts from time to time a humorous bon mot. Through being thus refreshed and renewed it becomes possible to be open to receive something spiritually new. Who was a master of this? Shakespeare, the archetypal dramatist. When everything was driving breathlessly in the highest tension towards the climax of the drama, he spiced a scene with a pinch of humour and the spectators could cope with a new tension through being thus refreshed. As a Russian, you have a golden humour; use it in the right moment and you will experience that your wonderful seeds will germinate even more successfully.

Günther Herrmann and Ursula Oermann

Visit to Allgäu

In the summer of 1996 Ursula Oermann and I were overjoyed to welcome our dear friend Sergei Prokofieff and his charming wife Astrid to our home in Buching, Allgäu.

On one of the glorious summer days we were favoured with an excursion into the mountains. The Tegelberg-Gondel railway took us past the castles of Neuschwanstein and Hohenschwangau and up to the top station. Then began the by no means simple ascent to the Branderschrofen (1880 m). At a turn of the stony path Sergei Prokofieff suddenly laid himself down on his front for about half an hour in order to be able to take in the deep valleys and the massive chains of mountains spread out around him. We waited. A little later at the cross on the summit, we all enjoyed the most beautiful view over mountains and valleys. When I wanted to photograph Sergei Prokofieff at the summit cross, he hesitated and said: 'This is made of aluminium!'; but then he understandingly gave his consent.

Throughout this memorable visit we were able to perceive him and his wife as especially dear friends. And alongside all the depths of anthroposophical conversation he also gave evidence of thoroughly youthful characteristics.

Our delight and admiration for both of them were greatly heightened by this visit.

Martina Hiemer

Koktebel

At a conference on Maximilian Voloshin in Koktebel in June 2004 I came to know Sergei Prokofieff from a very private and endearing side. I had previously known him only from lectures. With the greatest enthusiasm, he told us of his holidays in Koktebel as a young person and his becoming familiar with the figure of Voloshin and his unusual house, the great library and thereby also his initial acquaintance with the works of Rudolf Steiner.

The following day he took us to Maximilian Voloshin's grave on its lofty heights and then to Mount Karadak. He said with great resoluteness and conviction: 'Here you have the steppe landscape as in Galicia and there the oak woods and hills and mountains as in Greece!' The Greeks indeed believed that the entrance to the underworld was here beneath the grey-black craggy rocks of Karadak. Sergei Prokofieff was quite proud that the region that he so loved had the potential to manifest two such different and significant qualities. When he was in Koktebel he was youthful, carefree and happy in a way that I no longer experienced him later.

Wolfram Graf

Sergei Prokofieff's voice

When I read Sergei Prokofieff's writings, his voice always sounds behind them, this wonderfully sonorous voice, remarkably powerful and yet not insistently vibrating and pervaded with a slight Russian accent, together with the modest and at the same time convincing way that he enters the space. I am grateful to my destiny that I could come to know him.

Peggy Elliott

Sergei's secretary

...so it happened that one day I had my introductory conversation with Sergei Prokofieff. He invited me into his office, and through his friendly, calm manner something essentially human took place; I felt valued not for my qualifications but was in a conversation between two individuals. When I was introduced to his Goetheanum colleagues, he said on our way back to the office: 'We'll do this for 10 years.' I was somewhat surprised about this time indication, but thought no more about it.[30]

---

[30]This was at the beginning of 2002. Exactly 10 years later, emeritus status

Also after I had become his secretary, I often experienced such moments of collaboration, a common striving for something important where each played his or her part according to what was possible. Thus I remember how I was trying to insert a drawing into a text on the PC. Herr Prokofieff came into the office and looked over my shoulder to see how it was going; and I said to him that it was not so simple. Then he said, 'Let me have a try'; he sat down at my desk and got started. It isn't so simple, he said then and we both had to laugh. After a few attempts we managed to sort it out together.

After the death in 2005 of his Russian translator, Frau Ursula Preuss, he started dictating his texts in German. It was simpler and faster to write directly on the PC than in shorthand. But I very soon learned that it was impossible to ask Herr Prokofieff questions or make comments during the dictation. This had to be kept until later. His concentration was not to be interrupted.

Diana and Ruth Pauli

Some amusing stories

On a lighter note, a story about Sergei riding horses. Sergei was staying with us. My two teenage daughters, Ruth and Lucy, had ponies, so we thought it would be fun for Sergei to have a go at riding. Although he had been on a horse before he was certainly not a competent rider.

We decided he should ride one of the ponies, accompanied by Ruth. They were to ride together down to the bottom of a woodland track and then ride back up, past where we were waiting. I had said to Ruth, 'Be careful, and go slow; we must get Sergei to his next lecture in one piece!'

I was horrified to hear them galloping at speed up the track towards us, Ruth leading the way. I was wondering why she was leading at such a pace. As they rushed past us we heard Sergei shouting, 'Faster, faster!'

When I was a child, Sergei and Astrid came on holiday to the Lake District with my family one summer. There were the three children—

---

was conferred on Sergei Prokofieff for health reasons.

Daniel, me, and Lucy—plus my mother and father, and Sergei and Astrid. One day, the adults prepared a picnic lunch and we all walked to a lake to spend the afternoon swimming. Sergei and Daniel decided to go swimming straight away, while the other adults laid the picnic out and I sat in the grass a little distance away from them, looking out onto the lake. After a few minutes, I saw Sergei and Daniel stop and tread water towards the middle of the lake. Sergei turned to Daniel, chuckling, and I heard him say, 'Daniel, let's pretend I've drowned! I'll dive down under the surface and put you on my shoulders, and then you wave your arms in the air and shout out that I've drowned, OK?' Sergei took a deep breath, ducked under the surface, and lifted Daniel onto his shoulders. The next thing my parents and Astrid saw was Daniel hovering suspiciously at waist-level in the water, waving his arms in the air, shouting, 'Help, help! It's Sergei! He's drowned!' Realizing immediately what was going on, they all called out to Daniel, 'Oh dear, what a shame!' before Sergei emerged from the water, he and Daniel giggling like a pair of schoolboys.

Ingrid Mochner

Russian

Ingrid Mochner writes in a letter about an experience in the context of a lecture by Sergei O. Prokofieff:

After the lecture the request came from the audience that he should speak something in Russian. As far as I remember, it was the Foundation Stone Meditation. His voice rang out so powerfully with a full breath that the whole of Russia spoke, blew, almost stormed across to us powerfully and warmly like a mighty wave.—This is the Russian nature, this is Russia, the path to the next cultural epoch.

About the Contributors

Brief biographical details about the authors and the individuals named in the articles, as far as these are known:

ELENA ABRAMOVA, Russian violinist in Auckland, New Zealand.

CARINA VON BALTZ, 1922–2013, violinist, worked for many years at the Goetheanum.

KARL VON BALTZ, 1898–1987, violinist, worked for many years at the Goetheanum; 1956–1958 member of the Vorstand at the Goetheanum.

ABAN BANA, eurythmist and teacher at the Basel Rudolf Steiner School and at one of the Steiner schools in London, later worked in India.

DILNAWAZ BANA, curative eurythmist and eurythmist at the Lukas Clinic in Arlesheim, later worked in India.

STEFANIA BERGAMINI, born in Rome, translator, Waldorf teacher, worked initially in Italy, now in Tessin.

ANDREI BYELI, 1880–1934, Russian poet and writer, was from 1914 until 1916 working at the building site of the first Goetheanum.

VICTOR VICTOROVICH BYELI, 1928–1998, second husband of Sophia Prokofieva, stepfather of Sergei O. Prokofieff.

EVGENIYA VICTOROVNA BYELI, daughter from Victor Victorovich Byeli's first marriage.

ALEXANDER BLOK, 1880–1921, Russian poet.

HAGEN BIESANTZ, 1924–1996, studied classical archaeology, from 1966 until his death a member of the Vorstand at the Goetheanum.

SIMON BLAXLAND-DE LANGE is a translator, author and biodynamic gardener and a Council member of the Anthroposophical Society in Great Britain.

HANNES BLEIKER, 1920–2006, doctor.

JOHANNES BLEIKER, 1892–1991, doctor.

CHARLOTTE BLUME, 1922–2017.

GENNADI ALEXANDROVICH BONDAREV, 1936–2022, Russian anthroposophist from Moscow, later in Basel, author of philosophical and sociological books.

ZHENYA BONDAREVA, first wife of Gennadi Bondarev.

PYOTR ALEXANDROVICH CHAIKOVSKY, Russian anthroposophist, photographer and doctor, since 2020 country representative of the Anthroposophical Society in Russia.

KATYA CHEMBERDZHI, born in Moscow, studied composition, music theory and piano, has lived since 1990 in Berlin.

NIKOLAI KARLOVICH CHEMBERDZHI, composer, 1903–1948 and Sarah Alexandrovna Levina, 1906–1976, composer and pianist.

VALENTINA NIKOLAYEVNA CHEMBERDZHI, born in Moscow, philologist, translator, author of a biography of Lina Prokofieva, the first wife of the composer Sergei Sergeyevich Prokofiev, lives in Barcelona.

OLIVER CONRADT, leader of the Mathematical-Astronomical Section at the Goetheanum.

MARIE-FRANÇOISE CUVILLIER, 1950–2018, priest of The Christian Community, worked at the time in Bonn, finally in France.

JOHN DAVY, 1927–1984, lecturer and deputy principal of Emerson College in Forest Row, actively involved with the Anthroposophical Society in Great Britain.

GÜNTHER DELLSBRÜGGER, priest of The Christian Community.

ALEXANDER (SASHA) ALEXEYEVICH DEMIDOV, 1944–2021, Russian anthroposophist from Moscow.

ULRIKE DREW, piano teacher and pianist. German anthroposophist working in the south of France.

ELENA DOMRATSHOVA, Russian eurythmist working in Stuttgart.

PEGGY ELLIOTT, from 2001 until 2004 secretary of Sergei O. Prokofieff.

PYOTR ERSHOV, 1815–1869, Russian poet, dramatist.

LEONID EVGENYEVICH FEINBERG, 1896–1980, poet, painter, aesthetics and art historian. Father of Sophia Leonidovna Prokofieva, grandfather of Sergei O. Prokofieff.

SAMUIL EVGENYEVICH FEINBERG, 1890–1962, pianist, composer and author, professor at the Moscow Conservatory, brother of Leonid Feinberg and great-uncle of Sergei O. Prokofieff.

EDWIN FROBÖSE, 1900–1997, actor, publisher in Dornach.

EVA FROBÖSE, 1915–2015, eurythmist, publisher in Dornach.

EVA-MARIA GARBE, 1929–1996, Waldorf teacher.

MICHAELA GLÖCKLER, for many years leader of the Medical Section at the Goetheanum.

CAROLA GOHRING, participant in the conference with Sergei O. Prokofieff in New Zealand.

WOLFRAM GRAF, composer and author, living in Hof, Germany.

REBECCA McGRATH,

RUDOLF GROSSE, 1905–1994, 1956–1988 member of the Vorstand at the Goetheanum, from 1966 to 1984 as chairman.

SEVAK EDWARD GULBEKIAN is the Chief Editor of Rudolf Steiner Press and Temple Lodge Publishing, Forest Row, Sussex and also of Clairview Books.

ELISAVETA NIKOLAYEVNA GULBINA, Russian anthroposophist from Moscow.

LEV NIKOLAYEVICH GUMILYOV, 1912–1992, Russian scholar, translator, archaeologist, son of Anna Akhmatova.

JOHANNES HÄNDLER, 1930–2023, for many years an actor at the Goetheanum.

VERONIKA HÄNDLER, 1936–2011, mentioned in the book as the housemother of the student house at the Goetheanum in 1981.

MANFRED HEID, 1924–2013, music teacher, listener to Sergei O. Prokofieff's lectures.

GERARD HERMANS, Dutch anthroposophist.

GÜNTHER HERRMANN and URSULA OERMANN, a husband and wife from Allgäu, friendly with Sergei O. Prokofieff.

ROLF HERZOG, priest of The Christian Community in Basel.

PETER HEUSSER, lecturer emeritus for anthroposophical medicine at the universities of Witten-Herdecke and Bern.

URSULA HEUSSER, eurythmist in Dornach and Witten-Herdecke.

FRIEDRICH HIEBEL, 1903–1989, participant in Rudolf Steiner's courses in September 1924, poet, editor of the weekly periodical *Das Goetheanum*, from 1963 until his death member of the Vorstand at the Goetheanum.

MARTINA HIEMER, living in Munich, listener to Sergei O. Prokofieff's lectures.

DIETER HORNEMANN, priest of The Christian Community, for many years actively involved with The Christian Community in Russia and in Ukraine, living in Braunschweig.

LYUBA HUSEMANN, 1903–1990, priest of The Christian Community.

VLADISLAV IVONIN, 1944–2020, Waldorf teacher and painter near St Petersburg, later in Stuttgart and Heidelberg.

ANNIE JAHN, 1924–2004, Austrian anthroposophist who already in the 1970s established contact with anthroposophists in various towns and cities in the Soviet Union.

VAN JAMES, painter, author and teacher at the Honolulu Waldorf School. Chairman of the Anthroposophical Society in Hawaii.

LAZAR KAGANOVICH, 1893–1991, 1924–1957 member of the Central Committee of the Communist Party in the Soviet Union.

GIORGI KAVTARADSE, 1942–2024, born in Georgia, pioneer anthroposophist in Saint Peterburg in the Soviet Union as early as the 1960s. Philosopher, lecturer, university teacher in economics and history.

ROLF KERLER, 1941–2015, co-founder of the GLS community bank in Bochum, 1988–2002 member of the Vorstand and treasurer of the General Anthroposophical Society.

KARLA KINIGER, Hinterstoder (Austria) 1921–2014 (Edinburgh), Waldorf teacher, participated already from the 1970s in the anthroposophical groups in Moscow.

ARNE KLINGBORG, 1915–2005, artist, publicist, co-founder of the Rudolf Steiner Seminar in Järna.

ELSE KLINK, 1907–1994, eurythmist, founder of the Else Klink Ensemble in Stuttgart.

MARIYA VICTOROVNA KOROVINA (Mashenka, Masha), half-sister of Sergei O. Prokofieff from the second marriage of his mother, Professor of Mathematics at the University of Moscow.

NATASHA KOVALENKO, 1955–2008, Russian anthroposophist from Moscow.

VITALI SEMYONOVICH KOVALENKO, 1936–2013, Russian anthroposophist, photographer.

NADYEZHDA KRUPSKAYA, 1869–1939, revolutionary, wife of Vladimir Ilych Lenin.

CHRISTOPH LINDENBERG, 1930–1999, Waldorf teacher, historian, author of a biography of Rudolf Steiner.

ELENA LUTSHKINA, Russian anthroposophist and Waldorf teacher from Moscow.

PAUL MACKAY, met Sergei Prokofieff in 1982 in Bonn; from 2001 his colleague in the Vorstand at the Goetheanum.

ULRIKE MACKAY, studied Slavic languages, spent a term studying in Moscow, met Sergei Prokofieff before 1982, has been living in Dornach since 1997.

OSIP MANDELSTAM, 1881–1938, Russian poet.

REBECCA MCGRATH, born in 1964 in the USA, found Anthroposophy at age 33. She attended the English Study year under Virginia Sease. She strives to realize anthroposophy into the world.

VERA NIKOLAYEVNA MARKOVA, 1907–1995, philologist, translator of Japanese poetry and literary works, second wife of Leonid Feinberg, the maternal grandfather of Sergei O. Prokofieff.

MIRA (MARIYA-CECILIYA) ALEXANDROVNA MENDELSON, 1915–1968, second wife of Sergei Sergeyevich Prokofiev.

VSEVOLOD MEYERHOLD, 1874–1940, Russian actor and director.

INGRID MOCHNER, 1938–2021, listener to lectures by Sergei O. Prokofieff.

FABIO MONTELATICI, Waldorf and eurythmy teacher at the Scuola Steiner-Waldorf Colli near Padua, author of several books on anthroposophy in Italian.

BARBARA MRAZ, eurythmist working in Berlin.

BORIS NOSOV, 1949–1994, Russian anthroposophist from Moscow.

NICHOLAS NUNHOFER, living in Great Britain.

ULRICH OELSSNER, architect and painter in Dornach.

THOMAS O'KEEFE, founder of the newsletter *Deepening Anthroposophy*, collaborator of the Chadwick Library Press US as a translator and editor of Rudolf Steiner's works.

DIANA PAULI, colour-light therapist, English anthroposophist, actively involved with the School of Spiritual Science in Stourbridge.

ROGER PAULI, biodynamic farmer and innovator in the realm of industrial glass-manufacture, English anthroposophist, friend of Sergei Prokofieff.

RUTH PAULI, psychologist, English anthroposophist, daughter of Roger and Diana Pauli, lives in Birmingham.

TATYANA PETROVNA PIROGOVA, Russian anthroposophist in Arlesheim.

URSULA PREUSS, 1922–2005, Waldorf teacher, translator, until her death translated all Sergei O. Prokofieff's books into German, first journey to the Soviet Union in 1963, early meeting with the anthroposophical group in Moscow.

GABRIEL PROKOFIEV, son of Oleg Sergeyevich Prokofiev, half-brother of Sergei O. Prokofieff. Musician, composer and conductor in London.

LINA IVANOVNA PROKOFIEVA, née Carolina Codina, 1897–1989, first wife of the composer Sergei Sergeyevich Prokofiev.

OLEG SERGEYEVICH PROKOFIEV, 1928–1998, second son of the composer Sergei Sergeyevich Prokofiev. Painter and visual artist.

SERGEI SERGEYEVICH PROKOFIEV, 1891–1953, Russian composer and pianist.

SOPHIA PROKOFIEVA, NÉE FEINBERG, 1928–2025, mother of Sergei O. Prokofieff, poet, writer and illustrator of children's books, author of plays.

ALA BORISOVNA RAGOSHINA, Russian anthroposophist from Moscow.

EVA RATNOVSKY, 1928–2019, eurythmist.

RAOUL RATNOVSKY, 1912–1999, sculptor, founder of the Sculpture School at the Goetheanum.

GISELA REUTHER, 1924–2013, co-founder of the GLS community bank, Bochum, 1977–1993 member of the Vorstand at the Goetheanum, 1977–1988 treasurer of the General Anthroposophical Society.

FLORIAN RODER, 1958–2020, anthropsophist from Munich.

CLAUS-PETER RÖH, Waldorf teacher, former leader of the Pedagogical Section at the Goetheanum.

CARINA SCHMID, eurythmist, founder of the Hamburg Eurythmy School, former leader of the Eurythmy Ensemble at the Goetheanum.

MANFRED SCHMIDT-BRABANT, 1926–2001, anthroposophist from Berlin, from 1975 member of the Vorstand at the Goetheanum, from 1984 as chairman.

HEINRICH SCHNEIDER, 1929–2020, doctor, psychiatrist, worked before his retirement in the Bern area.

MARYETTA SHAGINYAN, 1888–1982, Russian-Armenian writer, aesthetics and art historian, journalist.

DMITRI SHOSTAKOVICH, 1906–1975, Russian composer.

ILONA SCHUBERT, 1900–1983, eurythmist at the Goetheanum.

VIRGINIA SEASE, 1935 born in Philadelphia. Graduate study in Germany and California, Ph.D.; Waldorf School teacher in Los Angeles; Council member of the AS in America; Executive Council member at the Goetheanum, 1984–2015; now emerita living in Dornach.

PETER SELG, doctor, psychiatrist, director of the Ita Wegman Institute in Arlesheim for basic research in anthroposophy, co-leader of the General Anthroposophical Section at the Goetheanum.

YURI IVANOVICH SENNIKOV, 1948–2010, Russian painter and anthroposophist.

HERBERT SEUFERT, 1927–2010, from the 1970s onwards regularly in Moscow for work with the anthroposophical groups there, Waldorf teacher and goldsmith. Father of Astrid Prokofieff-Seufert.

JÖRGEN SMIT, 1916–1991, Waldorf teacher, co-founder of the Rudolf Steiner Seminar in Järna, from 1975 until his death a member of the Vorstand at the Goetheanum.

MARJORIE SPOCK, 1904–2008, Waldorf teacher, eurythmist, biodynamic gardener and anthroposophist in the USA, met with Rudolf Steiner, participated in the Christmas Conference 1923/24.

IRINA SYRKOVA, anthroposophist from Moscow.

VLADIMIR (VOLODYA) GENNADIYEVICH TIKHOMIROV, 1941–2018, Russian anthroposophist.

OLIVIERA TODOROVIC, anthroposophist in Belgrade, Serbia.

GEORG UNGER, 1909–1999, mathematician, physicist; 1963–1990 leader of the Mathematical-Astronomical Section at the Goetheanum.

RUTH UNGER, 1909–2006, speech formation artist and actress at the Goetheanum.

CARINA VACA ZELLER, doctor in Santiago de Chile, representative of the Anthroposophical Society in Chile.

HARRIET FREIHN VON VACANO, 1862–1949, anthroposophist from the Baltic; early esoteric pupil of Rudolf Steiner, lived from 1900 in Germany.

ROBERT VEITENTHAL, had been living in Öhningen, Germany. Listener to lectures by Sergei O. Prokofieff.

KONSTANZE VOLBEHR, lives in Dornach. Listener to lectures by Sergei O. Prokofieff.

MARGARITA VOLOSHINA, née Sabashnikova, 1882–1973, Russian painter; collaborated in the building of the first Goetheanum, lived from 1924 onwards in Stuttgart.

MARIYA STEPANOVA VOLOSHINA, née Sabolotska, 1897–1976, second wife of Maximilian Voloshin, nurse.

MAXIMILIAN ALEXANDROVICH VOLOSHIN, 1877–1932, Russian poet, painter, 1914–1915 worked on the building of the first Goetheanum.

ELISABETH WAGNER-KOCH, 1923–2022, painter in Dornach.

GERARD WAGNER, 1906–1999, painter in Dornach.

KURT VON WISTINGHAUSEN, 1901–1986, priest and founding member of The Christian Community.

VLADIMIR ZHDANOV, 1902–1964, Russian general and group captain.

ALEXEI ZHUKOV, 1951–2016, Moscow journalist, writer, latterly country representative of the Anthroposophical Society in Russia.

MARINA TSVETAYEVA, 1892–1941, Russian poetess and author.

A note from the publisher